Gerasa and the Decapolis

DUCKWORTH DEBATES IN ARCHAEOLOGY
Series editor: Richard Hodges

Also available

Archaeology and Text
John Moreland

Beyond Celts, Germans and Scythians
Peter S. Wells

Combat Archaeology
John Schofield

Debating the Archaeological Heritage
Robin Skeates

Loot, Legitimacy and Ownership
Colin Renfrew

Origins of the English
Catherine Hills

The Roman Countryside
Stephen L. Dyson

Shipwreck Archaeology of the Holy Land
Sean A. Kingsley

Social Evolution
Mark Pluciennik

State Formation in Early China
Li Liu & Xingcan Chen

Towns and Trade in the Age of Charlemagne
Richard Hodges

Villa to Village
Riccardo Francovich & Richard Hodges

Gerasa and the Decapolis:

A 'VIRTUAL ISLAND' IN NORTHWEST JORDAN

David Kennedy

Duckworth

First published in 2007 by
Gerald Duckworth & Co. Ltd.
90-93 Cowcross Street, London EC1M 6BF
Tel: 020 7490 7300
Fax: 020 7490 0080
inquiries@duckworth-publishers.co.uk
www.ducknet.co.uk

© 2007 by David Kennedy

All rights reserved. No part of this publication
may be reproduced, stored in a retrieval system, or
transmitted, in any form or by any means, electronic,
mechanical, photocopying, recording or otherwise,
without the prior permission of the publisher.

A catalogue record for this book is available
from the British Library

ISBN-10: 0 7156 3567 0
ISBN-13: 978 0 7156 3567 4

Typeset by Ray Davies
Printed in Great Britain by
CPI Bath

Contents

Preface	8
Abbreviations	9
The Decapolis	10
Principal ancient and modern place-names	11
List of illustrations	12
1. Defining the topic	15
1.1. The topic	15
1.2. Study area	19
1.3. The problem	24
1.4. Conclusion	26
2. Evidence and methodologies	28
A. Evidence	28
2.1. Scale and survival	28
B. Methodologies	37
2.2. Archaeological interpretation and texts	37
2.3. Nomads	40
3. The natural and human landscape and environment	50
3.1. Introduction	50
3.2. A 'virtual island'	52
3.3. Broad patterns	55
3.4. Micro-regions: diversity and difference	62
3.5. Natural routes	74
3.6. Ancient climate and environment	77
3.7. Discussion	82

4. Settlement	84
4.1. Hellenistic beginnings, c. 300-50 BC	84
4.2. Early Rome, c. 50 BC – AD 200	85
4.3. Opening up the interior: communications and security, AD 200-350	88
4.4. A 'world of villages'… and churches, AD 350-600	95
4.5. Ruling from the margins, AD 600-850	100
4.6. Discussion	104
5. Population and people	108
A. Population size	108
5.1. Introduction	108
5.2. Population numbers	109
5.3. Northwest Jordan	113
5.4. Discussion	120
B. Application	123
5.5. Cemeteries	123
6. A world of writing	126
6.1. Introduction	127
6.2. Writing in the Near East	127
6.3. Greeks and Romans	128
6.4. The scale of writing	131
6.5. Visibility and use	138
6.6. 'Safaitic' inscriptions	143
6.7. Conclusion	147
7. The structures of the Roman state	151
7.1. The provinces	151
7.2. Provincial governors at work	156
7.3. Provincial administration	160
7.4. The Roman census	167
8. Everyday life	171
8.1. Health, disease and poverty	171
8.2. Seasonality of birth, marriage and death in the Decapolis	174

Contents

8.3. Occupations	176
8.4. Markets	179
8.5. Miscellaneous	180
9. Where to next?	185
A. Change	185
9.1. Overview	185
9.2. Explaining change	188
B. Data and analysis	191
9.3. Survey	191
9.4. Places	193
C. Interpretations	195
9.5. Nomads and traders	195
9.6. Arid-land farming	196
Bibliography	199
Index	211

Preface

The genesis of this book lies in three decades of fieldwork in northern Jordan, beginning with Qasr el-Hallabat and the Azraq Oasis in the mid-1970s and running through to survey beyond the walls of Gerasa today. An opportunity to put together the book itself was provided by a Membership and Summer Vistorship in the superb surroundings of the Institute for Advanced Study at Princeton in 2004-5 then by a Stanley J. Seeger Fellowship in Hellenic Studies at Princeton University in 2005-6. I am grateful to both those institutions for their incomparable support and facilities. In particular I would like to thank two of the many people whose support was crucial: Glen Bowersock and Dimitri Gondicas.

I would also like to thank Julie Kennedy for again preparing the illustrations, reading the text and habitual interest and support.

Abbreviations

Abbreviations employed for periodicals in the main Bibliography below are those recommended in the *American Journal of Archaeology* 95 (1991): 1-16. Others used in the text are as follows:

ABD = D.N. Freedman, G.A. Herion, D.F. Graf and J. Pleins (eds) *The Anchor Bible Dictionary,* New York, 1992, 6 vols
CIL = *Corpus Inscriptionum Latinarum,* Berlin, 1863-
IGLS = *Inscriptions grecques et latines de la Syrie,* Paris, 1929-
IGRR = *Inscriptiones Graecae ad Res Romanas Pertinentes,* Paris, 1911-1927
LCM = Long Classical Millennium
JBAP = Jarash Basin Archaeological Project
NWJ = Northwest Jordan
PES = Butler, H.C., et al. (1907-1949) *Publications of the Princeton University Archaeological Expeditions to Syria in 1905-1905 and 1909,* 4 vols in many parts, Leyden
Papyri from Dura Europus, Oxyrhynchus, and the Michigan, Yadin and Yale collections:
   P.Dura
   P.Mich.
   P.Oxy.
   P.Yadin
   P.Yale
Roxan, *RMD* = M. Roxan, *Roman Military Diplomas,* I-, London, 1978
SHAJ = *Studies in the History and Archaeology of Jordan,* vols I (1983)-VIII (2004): in progress
SHS = Southern Hauran Survey

The Decapolis

The name implies ten cities. In fact, the Elder Pliny (d. AD 79) tells us: 'Adjoining Judaea on the side of Syria is the region of the Decapolis, so-called from the number of its towns, though not all writers keep to the same list; most however include Damascus, with its fertile water-meadows that drain the river Chrysorrhoe, Philadelphia, Raphana (all these three withdraw towards Arabia), Scythopolis (formerly Nysa, ...) ...; Gadara, past which flows the river Yarmuk; Hippo [= Hippos] ..., Dion, Pella rich with its waters, Galasa [= Gerasa], Canatha' (*NH* 5.75, LCL trans. H. Rackham). Ptolemy's *Geography* (5.14.22), published in the early second century AD, lists eighteen names for 'Coelesyria and the Decapolis' together, including nine of those on Pliny's list: Damascus, Hippos, Gadara, Scythopolis, Gerasa, Pella, Dium, Philadelphia, Canatha). Three more on Ptolemy's list are commonly regarded as Decapolis cities: Capitolias, Adra [= Adraha] and Abila. The last of these is explicitly attested as a Decapolis city on an inscription (*IGRR* III: 1057). In short, we appear to have as many as thirteen Decapolis cities. One (Scythopolis) lies west of the R. Jordan and at least four (Raphana, Damascus, Canatha, Hippos) lie north of the Yarmuk. The largest group by far – seven or eight – lie in Northwest Jordan.

Principal ancient and modern place-names

ancient to modern		modern to ancient	
Abila	Qweilbeh	Amman	Philadelphia
Abila (Peraea)	Tell al-Kuffrein?	Beit Ras	Capitolias
Arbela	Irbid?	Beth Shean	Scythopolis
Adraha	Dera'a	Bosra	Bostra
Besimoth	Sweimeh?	Dera'a	Adraha
Bostra	Bosra	Hisban	Esbus
Capitolias	Beit Ras	Irbid	Arbela?
Esbus	Hisban	Jarash	Gerasa
Gadara	Umm Qeis	Madaba	Madaba
Gadora	Salt	Qweilbeh	Abila
Gerasa	Jarash	Salt	Gadora
Livias	Tell er-Rama	Sweimeh?	Besimoth
Madaba	Madaba	Tabaqat Fihl	Pella
Pella	Tabaqat Fihl	Tell al-Kuffrein	Abila (Peraea)?
Philadelphia	Amman	Tell er-Rama	Livias
Scythopolis	Beth Shean	Umm Qeis	Gadara

List of illustrations

Map of the Graeco-Roman Near East	14
Fig. 1.1. Northwest Jordan	16
Fig. 1.2. Qasr el-Hallabat – aerial view looking southeast	17
Fig. 2.1. Aerial view of Khirbet Khaw	32
Fig. 2.2. Aerial view of Umm el-Jimal	33
Fig. 3.1. Physical geography of Northwest Jordan	54
Fig. 3.2. The micro-regions of Northwest Jordan	56
Fig. 3.3. Aerial view of the Madaba Plain at Esbus (Hesban)	58
Fig. 3.4. (a) Rainfall pattern. (b) Soils	59, 61
Fig. 3.5. (a) Natural vegetation. (b) Agricultural areas	63, 64
Fig. 3.6. Planted areas for (a) wheat and olives; (b) barley and grapes	65, 66
Fig. 3.7. Aerial view of the Jarash Basin	69
Fig. 3.8. Photo of cross-walls in Northwest Jordan	73
Fig. 3.9. Cistern in Umm el-Quttein	74
Fig. 3.10. Concentrations of ancient cisterns	75
Fig. 3.11. Drainage basin of the Dead Sea	80
Fig. 4.1. Roman road from Bostra just northwest of Umm el-Quttein.	89
Fig. 4.2. Roman road network in Northwest Jordan	90
Fig. 4.3. Yajuz: aerial view	97
Fig. 4.4. Umm er-Resas: aerial view	97
Fig. 4.5. A rectilinear 'farm' in the Basalt Desert south of Umm el-Jimal	99
Fig. 4.6. Settlement patterns in the Southern Hauran	106

List of illustrations

Fig. 5.1. Map of Roman villages in Southern Hauran
    recorded by the PES   122
Fig. 7.1. The changing administrative boundaries of
    the southern Near East in the Roman period   153, 154
Fig. 7.2. The Nabataean kingdom   155

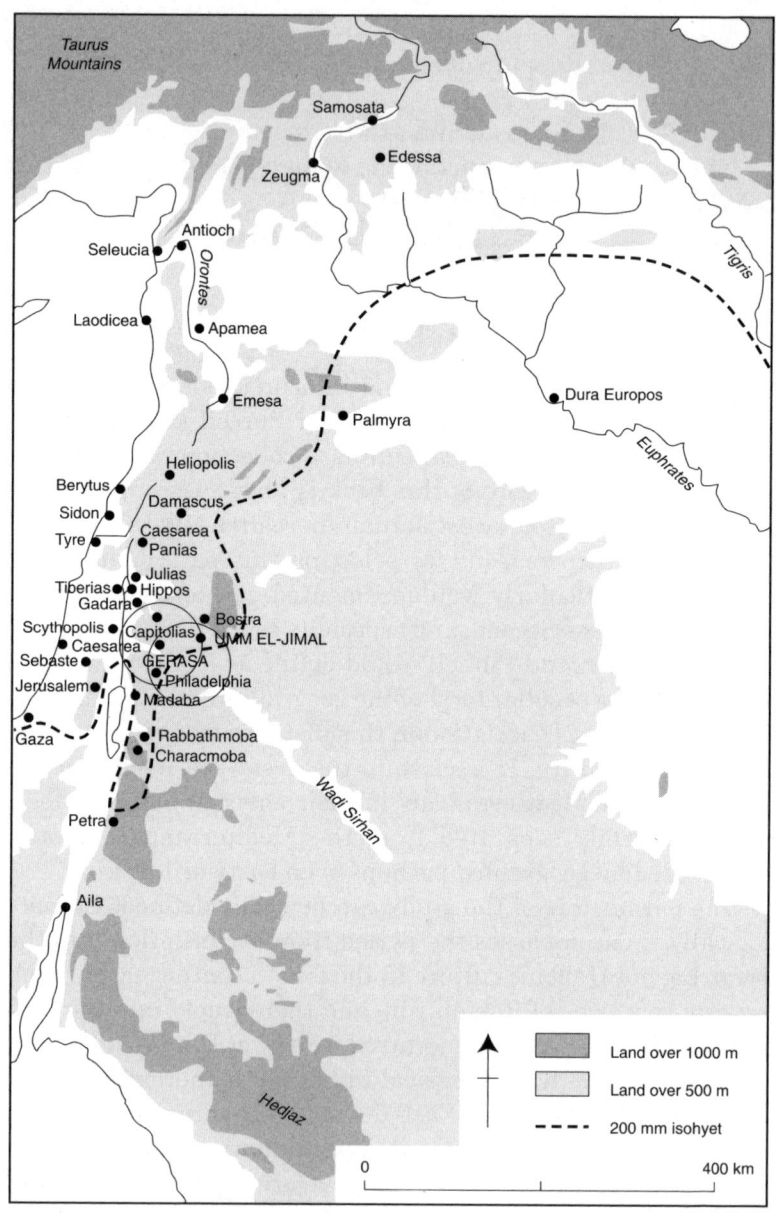

The Graeco-Roman Near East.

1

Defining the topic

1.1. The topic

In their massive exploration and interpretation of what they call *The Corrupting Sea,* Horden and Purcell (2004) persuasively define the Mediterranean as a collection of distinctive micro-regions. The core of this book is about a group of these micro-regions in Northwest Jordan (hereafter NWJ).

There are two reasons for selecting this particular group. First, it is particularly well-documented, not least by archaeological evidence. Second, and especially compelling, this region is what Horden and Purcell would define as a 'virtual island', isolated by the peculiar form of the geography and environment around it (ch. 3.2) – isolation in this instance fostering a highly distinctive identity. It is close to the great sea itself and the highlands are 'Mediterranean' in their environment and 'feel', yet it is firmly separated from the Mediterranean littoral, introverted by geography, perhaps even eastward-looking.

The parameters of the study can be easily defined. Chronologically it encompasses the period from the eruption into the Near East of Hellenic culture in the fourth century BC through several centuries of Roman rule and then deeply into the brilliant Umayyad civilization centred nearby at Damascus – what we may call the 'Long Classical Millennium' (hereafter LCM). Like much of the Near East during this period, the region enjoyed a long period of growth and dramatic spread of settlement to a degree not encountered before or to be seen again until the mid-twentieth century. Indeed, this settlement peak

Gerasa and the Decapolis

was to survive half a century longer in this region than elsewhere in the Near East (ch. 4.5).

The circles on Fig. 1.1 explain the boundaries (cf. ch. 3). Gerasa lies firmly in the highlands area, but within a 50 km radius are found at least eleven other ancient cities. Seven 'Decapolis' cities: Abila, Adraha, Capitolias, Gadara, Pella, Philadelphia and Scythopolis. Bostra, the provincial capital of the province of Arabia, is just a little further off, and to the west and south are Abila of the Peraea, Esbus, Gadora, Livias, and Madaba; Besimoth in the Peraea is also said to be a city. But this circle also shows graphically that while the urban world of NWJ is concentrated and embraces a network of cities, almost all of them lie in just one half of the circle. The eastern half encompasses a wide expanse of pre-desert (beginning broadly

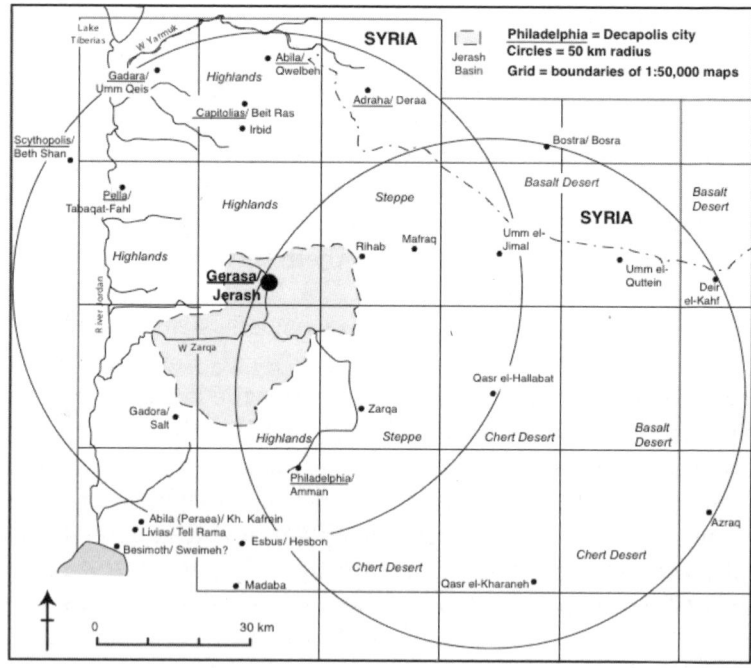

Fig. 1.1. Northwest Jordan.

1. Defining the topic

Fig. 1.2. Qasr el-Hallabat – aerial view looking southeast (APA97/ A6.06; 27 May 1997).

at Rihab) and reaches right out to the key site of Qasr el-Hallabat (Fig. 1.2).

Although the extensive ruins at Qasr el-Hallabat are intrinsically interesting, their location is yet more significant (ch. 4.5). Hallabat lies at the junction of pre-desert and desert but more than that it is at the point where two types of desert meet – the Basalt Desert and the Chert Desert (ch. 3).

The world of Gerasa as represented by the 50 km circle is a varied one – an extensive urban network, Jordan Valley, highlands and pre-desert. So, too, the world of the community that developed at Hallabat – in its orbit are three cities; Gerasa deep in a well-watered highland environment while Bostra and Philadelphia are in much more arid locations on the fringe of the desert. To the north of Hallabat is the fertile Southern Hauran, with its favourable rainfall. It has a thick scatter of villages and small towns, most notably Umm el-Jimal which grew to a third the size of Gerasa (Fig. 2.2). South of Hallabat lies a largely barren chert desert with little trace of human activity. From northeast to southeast and stretching as far as the Azraq Oasis the landscape is the rather different one of the Basalt Desert. Pockets of vegetation among the boulders offered attractions to man and beast, and shallow seasonal lakes are common still (ch. 3.5).

The archaeological record is a rich one in this Basalt Desert. Traces abound of temporary camps and in places people built houses and animal pens. They also constructed traps for the numerous gazelles that roamed the region in herds until recent times (below). Across the Basalt Desert as a whole these traps – known as 'kites' – run into the thousands; even in the small part encompassed by this study there are several hundred (ch. 4.5). And finally there are the thousands of graffiti, scratched on rock-faces and boulders across the same area (ch. 6.6). One cannot explain the urbanized highlands and thick settlement of the pre-desert without investigating, too, the widespread human presence and immense investment in the desert.

1. Defining the topic

The key to settlement everywhere in the wider region is water (ch. 3). But it also affected the routes that might be followed by both migrating nomads and traders linking the Gulf and Arabia with the Mediterranean world. Of course water was not an absolute determinant and in a few places human ingenuity was able to compensate for the deficiencies of nature. As we shall see (ch. 3.5), Hallabat is again at a key point on such routes and great efforts were expended in harvesting and storing water there.

1.2. Study area

Although the foregoing discussion in part explains the selection of this area for study, we must now step back and view the wider context.

In recent years there has been a rapid growth in research on the Near East – broadly the area from below the Taurus Mountains of southeastern Turkey to the start of the Arabian Desert. Sartre included the region in his massive *L'orient romain* (1991) and now there is his equally immense *D'Alexandre à Zénobie. Histoire du Levant antique IVe siècle av. J.-C. – IIIe siècle ap. J.-C.* (2001; rev. ed. 2003), the Roman part of which has now been translated into English and published as *The Middle East Under Rome* (2005). We also have Ball's provocative but unsettling *Rome in the East. The Transformation of an Empire* (2000) and Butcher's stimulating *Roman Syria and the Near East* (2003). Several books have dealt with aspects of Roman Palestine, and Bowersock's enduring and highly readable *Roman Arabia* (1983) remains fundamental for that province despite the barrage of new research it provoked. Others have looked at major aspects of the region – Isaac's *The Limits of Empire: The Roman Army in the East* (1992) and Pollard's *Soldiers, Cities, and Civilians in Roman Syria* (2000), and the essays collected in Isaac's *The Near East Under Roman*

Rule (1998), Graf's *Rome and the Arabian Frontier: from the Nabataeans to the Saracens* (1997) and MacAdam's *Geography, Urbanisation and Settlement Patterns in the Roman Near East* (2002). Finally, and especially important, is the first part (to AD 337) of Millar's projected two-volume history, *The Roman Near East* (1993). This is a massive work of synthesis and stimulating interpretation, evoking the depth, scale and shear richness of the region, and underscoring the uniqueness of the Roman centuries: great cities with a wealth of public buildings and rich art and architecture, immense temples, forts, roads, are all there in abundance. Finally, the relevant chapters of two books of air photographs vividly evoke the landscapes and places of the Near East (Gerster and Wartke 2003; Kennedy and Bewley 2004).

Three major themes are central to research. First, the astonishing number, scale and variety of settlements and the unparalleled extent of their spread. Second, Millar observed that what all the successive sub-regions of the Near East had in common, as one moved south from the Euphrates, was the pre-desert beyond (1993: 387). It is easy, when focussing on the rich texture of civilization in the region, to overlook the fact that the looming arid lands and the nomad beyond are no mere spectators to the great dramas acted out in the arable lands.

Finally, for twenty years, Shahid has been exploring 'Rome and the Arabs' as the theme of a succession of books (1984a; 1984b; 1989; 1995) which underscore the significance of the native population, including the nomad. Others – not least Ball (2000) – have also done much to place the subsequent seizure of the entire region by Islamic Arab armies in context and remind us always to look beyond the arable lands. Nomads on the fringes of great empires interact with and powerfully influence the civilized state to a surprising degree. They can at different times be inside the frontier on seasonal migration, engaged in trade, drawn in through imperial expansion, a significant source of military manpower or at war with their great neigh-

1. Defining the topic

bour. The powerful lesson, however, is that one should not see them as a people *beyond* the frontier.

How best, and where, may we explore these phenomena – the impressive settlement extent of the Roman-period peoples and the relationship between the 'desert and the sown'? I concluded a review of Millar's *The Roman Near East* with suggestions for archaeological research which could make a significant contribution to developing our understanding of what Millar had called 'communities and culture' (Kennedy 1999). Principally we needed 'an integrated research programme' focussing on a single broad area extending across the major geographical and environmental zones of the Near East – arable highlands, pre-desert and desert. In short, we should look at a single micro-region or group of them. Even in 1999, in terms of opportunity, access, existing data, quality of preservation and compactness, one region seemed especially well-suited – NWJ (and parts of adjacent Syria) from the Jordan Valley and the Highlands of Ajlun through the Southern Hauran to the Basalt and Chert Deserts beyond around the Azraq Oasis.

This suggestion was subsequently developed further and the case made more firmly in a series of publications. De Vries' book on the well-preserved Nabataean-Roman-Early Islamic town of Umm el-Jimal in the Southern Hauran provided the context for a detailed interpretation of the air photographic evidence for a wide area of the surrounding landscape (Kennedy 1998a). Second, a seminar on *Identities* was the opportunity to bring an archaeological approach to the study of the cultural identity of Gerasa (Kennedy 1998b). Finally, 'The frontier of settlement in Roman Arabia. From Gerasa to Umm el-Jimal ... and beyond' (Kennedy 2000), linked these two and pursued them into the desert beyond.

In light of all these, I returned (2004a) to the proposal made in the Millar review (above) with a paper setting out the detailed case for a multi-period, multi-disciplinary study of a region of the Near East. The present book is in part a further working out of these ideas, through essays to enrich our understanding of the region and stimulate further research.

Several other works have underscored the enormous potential of synthesis of wide-ranging data: First, Barker et al.'s superb study (1996) arising from fieldwork in Libya – *Farming the Desert* (reviewed: Kennedy 2001a). Second, Hirschfeld's stimulating survey of 'Farms and villages in Byzantine Palestine' based upon the detailed surveys of the archaeological remains over a wide area (1997) and his earlier study of *The Palestinian Dwelling* (1995). Third, the challenging insights in Horden and Purcell's (2000) major re-interpretation of Mediterranean history which helped define the choice made here and infused much of the thinking in this book as a whole.

In proposing this region out of a number that might have been selected, it is its *positive* advantages which explain why other possibilities have been passed over: we can study a network of closely spaced and well-explored cities; a significant number of smaller settlements has been investigated; there have been several major intensive multi-period ground surveys; there is a considerable corpus of written material; the infrastructure of communications is extensive and quite well-known; geography and environment are highly varied within a still compact area; air photographic interpretation and aerial reconnaissance are relatively well-developed; and the great slash of the Rift Valley isolates the urban heart of NWJ and separates it from the Mediterranean, leaving it balanced between 'the desert and the sown' and making it a highly distinctive region, a 'virtual island'.

The region is not perfect. A glaring omission from among so much fieldwork there is the fundamental analysis and interpretation of the ancient environment and its potential as a guide to the What and Why of every period (although there are beginnings which can be exploited: see 3.7). Equally startling in

1. Defining the topic

an area in which ground survey has been so extensive, is the absence of a survey around Gerasa itself, the best explored of all the Decapolis cities.

In the pages that follow, the cities are prominent, as they should be: numerous and well-preserved structures, sometimes decades of excavation and a score of monographs. The Decapolis cities and their neighbours form a natural network, close to one another and at the same time almost isolated by nature from their further neighbours. In urban terms alone the micro-region is a treasure house of places and published material (cf. 9.3).

But prominent too in these chapters are many other places whose very names will be unknown to most readers though they are significant archaeological sites. Few, for example, will have heard of the small ruined town of Umm el-Jimal, yet we have numerous buildings, some with walls three storeys high; ground plans of its 128 houses – at Gerasa we have a single example (from the Umayyad period); it is the source of over 500 inscriptions in four languages – about the same number as for Gerasa; and, like Gerasa, it has 15 churches. The modern village of Hayyan al-Mashrif (fortunately) encircles the extensive ruins of a small town whose very existence was barely known 25 years ago yet includes several churches, one with the otherwise rare Aramaic language of the sixth and seventh century AD called Syro-Palestinian or 'Melkite' in its mosaic floor (ch. 4.4). Rihab nearby has another 15 churches, two of them including mosaics dating just before the Islamic conquest. Khirbet es-Samra is a small town extensively excavated over many years to reveal numerous churches, a Roman fort and a cemetery distinguished above all by several dozen epitaphs in Syro-Palestinian (ch. 6.3). And there are dozens more of such small settlements to complement and provide a rural context for the cities.

The region as a whole is criss-crossed with Roman roads and traces of ancient tracks, while aerial photographs have revealed thousands of 'sites' and extensive areas of fossilised field boundaries.

Above all, perhaps, there is a wonderful and varied landscape. One does not need to subscribe to any rigid deterministic view of geography or environment to recognize that these were enormously influential forces in shaping the place and period (ch. 3). And what a period! Never before had the region been as urbanized and as densely and extensively settled. Nor was it again to reach such levels until the twentieth century – perhaps not till the 1950s.

We know a great deal already about this region with its network of cities, its mass of data from ground surveys and aerial reconnaissance, the extensive work done on such categories as roads and military sites and of course its unexpectedly considerable documentary evidence. The database is large and varied, significant and inviting. Yet it is plainly inadequate. We have volume rather than quality at times, and much of what we have is undigested. We *know* a great deal but we *understand* relatively little about population, cultural identity, the dynamics of change, relationship to a wider world, and much else.

1.3. The problem

It remains to reflect on the nature of research in this region and in the wider Near East. Classical Archaeology in general has long been viewed as old-fashioned (Dyson 1989; 1993) but in recent years both Classical and Near Eastern Archaeology have shifted significantly in methods and approaches. Indeed, many Classical Archaeologists are no longer Classicists by training and much of the evidence for Classical Archaeology is today produced by fieldworkers who are simply 'archaeologists' operating as professionals without necessarily any attachment to a particular period or place.

In part the change is due to the development of ground

1. Defining the topic

survey as a significant technique alongside excavation. Surveyors cannot simply select their period of interest; every site of every period must be recorded and the technique obliges the surveyor to view *every* period in its chronological context and to contemplate the wider sweep of history. Ground survey (and the related techniques of remote sensing, especially Aerial Archaeology) forced all archaeologists to see their period of interest in a wider timeframe, and to develop collaborative approaches.

Of course, the stimulating interpretations of Barker and others (ch. 1.2) are not only the outcome of a novel technique, multi-period projects, interdisciplinary collaboration and an explicitly deductive approach. For some periods these would have been of limited value if they had not been able to draw on the decades of intensive work by others, not least Classicists and Classical Archaeologists, in plodding textual analysis, excavations and thankless but vital cataloguing. Nor was it only outside forces at work on Classical Archaeology. The past generation has seen significant shifts in the study of Greek and Roman history and the integration into the subject of the methods and objectives of the Social Sciences. Some of the most exciting work being done today in the study of the Greek and Roman world is in such subject areas as ecology, health and disease, demography, slavery, literacy, acculturation, and so on (Sauer 2004).

This brings us back to the East and to the Near East in particular. Despite the relative neglect of the region and cyclical pattern of such research as there was, cumulatively a great deal *has* been done and significant publications have sought to generalize from and interpret it. To some extent, however, the efforts have had limited results. So much of what is known is skewed in type or inadequately digested, and the modernization of Near Eastern Archaeology and of Classical Archaeology in the Near East has been uneven and limited. In a nutshell, there is enormous potential because of the quality of survival and the abundant evidence; on the other hand, it is poorly understood, seldom collected and analysed as one needs, and heavily distorted by a long tradition of focus on cities and their public buildings, on military sites and Roman roads.

The situation cannot be changed overnight, and it is important to recognize that even with new approaches and focuses, the existing data remains an immense and under-exploited resource. And not just the archaeological evidence. The written evidence, the 'texts', are a wonderful resource (ch. 6). And there is more still. We know an immense amount about the Roman world as a whole and how it worked (chs 7, 8). We know a great deal not just about the cities of the Near East, but about urbanism in the Roman empire, from which to derive insights, parallels and contrasts. And likewise with roads, forts, the Roman army and warfare, the economy, empires – all of these and more are being researched on an empire-wide scale or indeed beyond the limits of just Rome and have the potential to feed into analysis and interpretation in this particular 'virtual island'.

1.4. Conclusion

Despite the prominence of the cities, this book is not 'about' Gerasa or Pella or Madaba or Bostra. Rather it is about the region as a whole. It is a series of essays exploring *how* it may be studied by investigating some aspects of the region. A particular objective is to give some colour to a region as a whole for which we have so much evidence but too little understanding of what it was like, why it was like that and how and why it developed and changed.

The following chapters are not intended to be definitive; indeed, all could be expanded extensively and one – 'Settlement' – is the subject of a major study now in progress. The intention is to enrich our understanding of the region and stimulate

1. Defining the topic

research with the objective of achieving a holistic and diachronic interpretation of a key region. The data is abundant and much more is being digested for preparation. Yet more will be produced in the future. Some of the latter will be the by-product of development. More should be the outcome of targeted fieldwork and research. Just what that should be will be returned to in ch. 9.

*

Finally, a caveat. Some of the features and themes discussed below run throughout the LCM; others are shorter-lived. Some of the generalizations may apply to the entire period; more commonly they refer only to the short period defined there. We may, for example, talk of the Roman census in the early imperial period with a degree of confidence; for the subsequent centuries a quite different process was at work.

2

Evidence and methodologies

> Tyche has skewed our evidence with malice and thoroughness.
> Horsfall 1991: 67

A. EVIDENCE

2.1. Scale and survival

Most of what was written in the Long Classical Millennium is lost irrevocably. What survives is a small and biased selection. Perishable materials (parchment, papyrus, wood) were undoubtedly the commonest medium of written communication running into billions of items across the period for the Near East alone. These have been almost entirely lost with just a few tens of thousands surviving, almost entirely from Egypt. Inscriptions and graffiti on imperishable materials (stone, metal, ceramics, glass, bone) were far less common – perhaps hundreds of millions – but inevitably survive rather better with a few hundred thousand examples. Painted texts (on wood, stone, plaster, glass etc.), though once very common, will seldom survive, while those made of stone or glass cubes spelling out words in a mosaic will be more fortunate. It is not just a matter of the durability of the material on which the writing was done. The recycling of inscribed bronze tablets or precious metals was frequent and was an entirely destructive process; inscriptions on stone were less frequently re-used and the process was less destructive – texts may be damaged or hidden from sight but seldom obliterated. Finally, in the case of literature, the

2. Evidence and methodologies

expense and difficulty of making multiple copies makes such texts unlikely to survive; on the other hand repetitive copies of, for example, tax receipts, will survive in seemingly large numbers. Moreover, it is by and large the everyday that is most vulnerable thereby privileging at least some of the more public and considered texts. Next, writing – or at least inscribing – seems to have enjoyed a period as a fashion ('the epigraphic habit') which was unrelated to general levels of literacy or wealth – people erected tombstones and inscribed public dedications in the first three centuries AD to an extent not seen before or later.

A visitor to the Near East exploring the archaeological remains of its Graeco-Roman past soon encounters an insuperable problem: the staggering quantities of structures and sites. Beyond the cities lie towns, villages, forts, roads, quarries. Artefacts survive in enormous numbers and great variety in public and private collections and in astonishing numbers on the surface of sites. Commonest everywhere is pottery, and we need only recollect the estimated six million sherds dumped by ancient potters in the rooms of the disused hippodrome at Jarash to grasp how immense is the database. However, what we have or can still see is but a small part of what survives but is mainly hidden from sight beneath the surface or below later structures. Likewise, what survives in total – visible and hidden – is itself a tiny part of what once existed. In short, in any analysis and interpretation of the ancient evidence we are dealing with a minute sample. Although Classical Archaeologists are indisputably better served than their colleagues in most other periods and places by the volume and range of evidence, it is salutary to recollect how small the assemblage is and that it is not representative. Let me illustrate these points through a handful of examples.

Gerasa and the Decapolis

Theatres, circuses and amphitheatres

A visitor to Jarash will be struck not least by the two great theatres, immensely impressive in their scale and preservation even before modern consolidation and reconstruction. There is another well-preserved pair at Amman (Philadelphia), two at Umm Qeis (Gadara) and two more at Beth Shean (Scythopolis). Theatres are in fact common in the Decapolis and perhaps that should not surprise us (see Table 4.1). Theatres are among the largest public buildings of Classical Antiquity and in this region they were often cut into a hillside – rather than free-standing – thereby helping to ensure their survival. It *should* be difficult to lose all trace of a theatre. And yet it *is* possible. At Gadara, much of the stonework of the large North Theatre was robbed out long ago and it would have required only a modest growth of the modern village to overflow and totally hide it. At Abila and Pella the traces of the theatres are modest. Much more instructive is the recent discovery of an otherwise unknown large theatre at Beit Ras (Capitolias). There, despite only a small modern village, little of the ancient town was known to scholars. Yet in 2002, development on the edge of the hill on which the core of the village stood, exposed part of an immense theatre totally buried and hidden within the 'hill'. This cautionary tale is reversed at Bostra. There the theatre became the core of an Islamic fortress and consequently is one of the best-preserved in the Near East. On the other hand, the hippodrome at Bostra, though long known, is poorly preserved and it is only very recently that the traces were found of an amphitheatre. Once again, a huge monumental structure *had* disappeared from view.

The lesson to be drawn is that there is abundant scope for such structures to be lost. The known theatre at Pella is small and we should expect to find a second, large theatre there, too, in future. We may ultimately find second theatres at Abila and

2. Evidence and methodologies

Capitolias as well. Adraha was rapidly re-developed in late Ottoman times and much was lost – including the theatre whose existence is known now only from a recently published old photograph (Frézouls 1989: 400, Fig. 111). And what about Gadora (Salt)? No trace of a theatre has ever been reported there. That place, however, remained a significant settlement and centre of government through to early British times, and its ancient remains were certainly dismantled and covered over to a degree not experienced at such places as Gerasa and Pella. Of course, non-Greek Gadora may never have had a theatre and that may be true as well of Madaba and Esbus, while Livias, Abila of the Peraea and Besimoth were probably too small and poor. Although it is not very likely that any city of NWJ besides Bostra had a purpose-built amphitheatre, the oddly-shaped example at Scythopolis is reminiscent of what the hippodrome at Gerasa looked like after re-modelling, so we should keep an open mind (Weiss 1999: 34-43). Finally, at Philadelphia we have two superb theatres but no circus/ hippodrome. In view of their commonness elsewhere in the region that is a surprise; as Philadelphia was renowned for its horse-breeding, it is probable there was once a circus (MacAdam 1992: 30; Graf 1997c: V, 267).

Forts

Roman forts abound in NWJ. Few have been excavated, but, fortunately, many can be dated in some respect through the survival of building inscriptions. Indeed, the preponderance of such inscriptions in Jordan comes precisely from this region (see Table 4.4) (Kennedy 2004b: 25-6). One thinks immediately of the tall walls and impressive towers of the fort at Deir el-Kahf or the forts and towers in and around the Azraq Oasis and the building inscriptions found with them (Kennedy 2004b: chs 7 and 8). And there are many more. In contrast, however, are the 'invisible' or lost forts. Khirbet Khaw was known to

Gerasa and the Decapolis

Fig. 2.1. Aerial view of Khirbet Khaw (APA05/ 7.22; 3 October 2005).

early visitors a century ago but described so poorly that its character and significance went unrecognised. Half a century ago or more it disappeared inside the enclosure of a Jordan Army camp, largely preserved – indeed frozen – in its condition because it was thus protected from routine pillaging or local development (Kennedy 2004b: 101-2). Yet there it stands still, 'rediscovered' on aerial photographs (Fig. 2.1) and looking remarkably similar in overall size and design to the probably contemporary fort at Umm el-Jimal (Fig. 2.2). At the latter, discovery was delayed until 1981 not because of lack of interest in the site but *despite* the extensive work there of the Princeton Expedition a century ago, numerous visitors since then and the major fieldwork of an American team at the site since 1972.

In contrast to these two places we have Qaryat el-Hadid, 8 km southwest of Khirbet Khaw. There, early travellers had noted, briefly and without much enthusiasm, an archaeological site east of the Roman highway, the *Via Nova Traiana,* just

2. Evidence and methodologies

Fig. 2.2. Aerial view of Umm el-Jimal (APA98/ 6.30; 12 May 1998).

Gerasa and the Decapolis

beside the River Zarqa. The site is now overlain by a suburb of modern Zarqa – fields, gardens, a school and mosque and a bus station – and can easily pass unnoticed. An old German air photograph of 1918, however, captured a large part of the site from above with the outline of what is clearly a major site – apparently a fort and a walled town (Kennedy 2002; 2004b: 105-7). Finally there is the fort at Umm el-Quttein, long implied by an altar erected by an auxiliary regiment but not traced till spotted on an old air photograph a generation ago (Kennedy and Riley 1990: 141-3).

Inscriptions

With limited literary sources, inscriptions have long been the object of intense activity, offering a further, complementary source of written evidence (and not just for what the words say: see ch. 5). So it is worthwhile exploring their survival. Let us look at the epigraphic finds from the other city sites of NWJ. The relevant volume of the corpus of Greek and Latin inscriptions for the area encompassing Amman and a wide area around (*IGLS* XXI), ran to only 184 inscriptions. Of these, despite the considerable size of ancient Philadelphia and its thousand-year history, just 38 inscriptions came from the Graeco-Roman city. At Salt (ancient Gadora), the total was one. Bostra has 472 (as of *IGLS* XIII in 1982). The corpus covering the other cities is in preparation (Gatier, personal communication) but the totals for those places are modest: Gadara: *c.* 59, Capitolias: *c.* 12 and Abila: *c.* 33.

At Jarash, all the early visitors since Seetzen in 1806 were interested in the visible Greek and Latin inscriptions and made transcriptions, drawings and later photographs. From early in the 1920s fieldwork commenced on the site and many more inscriptions were found on the surface or unearthed in excavations. When Kraeling's major book on *Gerasa* appeared in 1938,

2. Evidence and methodologies

it included 361 inscriptions (Welles at Kraeling 1938: 353-494). The total is impressive, but what does it really represent?

First, when that corpus was published in 1938, about a fifth of the texts had already disappeared and were known to the compiler only from copies made by earlier visitors. Of course, new inscriptions are being found there regularly: some 200 more since 1938 (Gatier, personal communication). Next, there is the remarkable site of Umm el-Jimal, a small ancient town in the Southern Hauran (4.4; 5.3). The Princeton Expedition publications on the site included no less than 291 inscriptions in Latin (5) and Greek (286) (*PES* III.A.3); more have been published intermittently over the years and a further crop in process of being edited runs to c. 140 in Greek (Graf, personal communication). Finally, Bauzou's collection (1998) of the whole or fragmentary Latin milestone inscriptions from the major highway from Bostra to Philadelphia has 157 texts from its 53 Roman miles.

A final observation, from work done in Israel. When the two main corpora of Greek (*IGRR*) and Latin (*CIL*) inscriptions were published (1911-27 and 1873), they contained a total of 0 and 3 respectively for the city of Caesarea Maritima. Since then several hundred inscriptions have been found, mainly in the excavations. The recently published corpus by Lehmann and Holum (2000) lists 411 inscriptions as of 1992 (no less than 204 previously unpublished) and over 200 more have been found since (Haensch 2002). The numbers are impressive and tell us a great deal about survival of evidence. But Isaac (2003: 666) underscores the limitations of such evidence in relation to Caesarea: despite the more than 600 now available, not one mentions the founder of the city (Herod the Great) and only one belongs to the period before AD 69 when the city was founded and the mass of construction took place. A significant number are in Latin and reflect the presence of governor, procurator and troops, but almost nothing sheds any light on or even mentions the other major feature of the city – the great harbour that made it a regional wonder. The numbers can be instructive. At Caesarea and Bostra the proportion of funerary inscriptions is about 50%; at Jarash about 12% (46 of the 361 inscriptions recorded by Kraeling). Although the number and proportion is relatively small, is this just the accident of survival? We might note, for example, that not one of these 46 epitaphs at Jarash is figured although figured tombstones are quite common further north. Perhaps we are seeing not just a different fashion in type of commemoration but in commemoration itself.

Two lessons are that the epigraphic harvest in NWJ is the richer for the long delay in the re-development of the area and that excavation has already revealed and will continue to produce significant numbers of additional texts. A hint of that is evident at Umm el-Jimal (above) but even more so at Khirbet es-Samra *c*. 35 km northeast of Amman, where excavation recovered part of a very poor cemetery but one marked by no less than 148 simple inscriptions, over half in rare Syro-Palestinian (chs 1.2; 6.3) (Humbert and Desreumaux 1998: 435-510 (Desreumaux)). What may we infer about inscriptions as a category of evidence in the region? Even now we have some 2000-3000 published inscriptions, several times as many are known and in various stages of publication, and we may suppose this still only represents a small fraction of those surviving but still to be found.

*

The loss of texts inscribed on stone is startling enough and apparently large scale. As we shall see, however, the loss of perishable material is almost total. Without looking further than written materials, we may cite the million or more census returns for the entire province that have been lost – bar one (see

2. Evidence and methodologies

7.4)! For the period from AD 106 to 235 the c. 10,000 soldiers of the army of Arabia were each given a pay record every three months: a total of c. 5,000,000 items. We have none (cf. Fink 1971: 242 and below, ch. 6.4).

B. METHODOLOGIES

Few ancient historians today rely on 'letting the evidence speak for itself'. Even where it is most abundant, data remains fragmentary, uneven and often ambiguous. In the case of NWJ, despite the quantities, variety and quality of the evidence, any 'history' of the region must turn elsewhere for evidence and insights. First, in the context of the Roman empire we have the enormous benefit of an entity that endured for several centuries and extended over an immense area. This goes some way to mitigate the fragmentary evidence for any given region or period because there are broad similarities which may be applied between a place or time of relatively abundant evidence to another where it is thinner or non-existent. Second, there is the evidence from outside the Graeco-Roman world and outside the period.

2.2. Archaeological interpretation and texts

It is not enough to interpret and explain the archaeological evidence, no matter how varied and abundant. Without an understanding of how the Roman empire functioned, how may we properly interpret the material culture? For example, an archaeologist may easily infer from the archaeological evidence the existence of a great Mediterranean-wide empire beginning in the last centuries BC and spanning several centuries. The existence of the uniquely rich remains of a great city in west-central Italy, bigger and grander by far than anything else around the Mediterranean for centuries, would doubtless suggest the political centre of this empire. There may be widely scattered badges of empire: regal symbols (such as ruler portraits and coin images); uniform units of measurement (such as the employment of Roman feet) in what would be identified as state buildings (administrative structures, forts, etc.) and the uniform size of land division systems (centuriation), in several widely separated parts of the Mediterranean world. The broad uniformity of the road system and the particular pattern it forms would imply that one is dealing with a centrally administered entity and the network extent would suggest the area (cf. Renfrew and Bahn 2004: 213).

The archaeologist could plausibly go on to infer the inevitable subdivision of a large territorial empire into smaller administrative units and the delegation of government. But how would divisions be recognized, what basis for division would be inferred and would alterations, even quite large ones, be recognized? The variety of systems of provincial government is potentially wide and would surely be very difficult to infer. Within such local units what impact did the imperatives of local administration bring about and in what ways did it affect the previous pattern? Does it matter or is this merely reflective of the interests of historians in politics and government and of little real importance to the preoccupations of archaeologists? It does matter, and we may illustrate the point more simply by reference to the direct impact imperial intervention could or might make at particular places.

Lepcis Magna and Gerasa

A purely archaeological interpretation of the city of Lepcis Magna in Libya would undoubtedly provide the broad chronology for a city growing, developing and ultimately reaching a remarkable level of prosperity and elaboration, a city spread over some 400 ha and including an impressive and largely

2. Evidence and methodologies

artificial harbour. These hard facts would probably be explained in terms of the rich agricultural hinterland where the traces of olive production could be seen not just in the arable lands of the coastal plain and on the adjacent plateau but even in the oil presses of the small farms in the water deficit lands beyond (Barker et al. 1996). The great harbour would have allowed the inference of significant 'trade' in oil and perhaps exotic commodities from sub-Saharan Africa. However, texts, mainly inscriptions, provide specific dates and groupings of dates for particular public buildings revealing phases of development from initial Punic settlement to the third century AD. The last of these came *c.* AD 200 and created an immense city seemingly out of proportion to what one would have inferred from the resources available to the place. Literary sources show that this last was the result of purely external *political* factors – Lepcis Magna was the hometown of the Emperor Septimius Severus (AD 193-211) and of his powerful praetorian prefect and kinsman, Plautianus. The entire imperial family visited Lepcis in 202-3, the first visit ever by a reigning emperor. Collectively and individually they lavished money on construction. There are parallels for similar generosity and the distortion of the archaeological evidence: Italica in Spain (home of two successive emperors, Trajan and Hadrian [AD 98-137]: Cassius Dio 69.10.1; Keay 1988: 59, 123-4) and the little town of Shahba in southern Syria transformed into Philippopolis (home of the Emperor Philip [AD 244-9]: Freyberger 1992). Without such knowledge how would we explain the sudden growth and development of such places? How, too, would we explain the rapid growth of Athens in the early second century AD if we did not know of Hadrian's great attachment to the place, his residence there on at least two occasions and his enormous benefactions to it (Thompson 1987: 9-14).

No emperor came from NWJ. On the other hand, as is well-known, Hadrian travelled extensively – perhaps for twelve

Gerasa and the Decapolis

years of his 21-year reign. There was a cultural expectation that rulers in the Roman world would give gifts to places in which they stayed for more than just a transit visit. Hadrian's journeys took him through northern Jordan, and we know – from a single inscription, now lost – that he resided at Gerasa; indeed, he may have spent an entire winter there (129/30). We have no explicit evidence for imperially funded construction at Gerasa as an outcome; what we do have is the evidence for a surge in construction of all kinds in the mid- and later second century. The surge is not confined to Gerasa – though most fully attested there (Table 2.1). It is probable, too, that it reflects not just the continued elaboration and development of the cities of the region that had been in progress for a century but the presence of the emperor giving an impetus to an existing process of monumentalization by local elites.

2.3. Nomads

A dominant feature of the Near East is the presence of nomads alongside the settled population; indeed, among and interacting with them. They are mentioned at an early point in Roman involvement in the first century BC and scattered references reveal their continued but shadowy presence over the next three centuries. It is only in the third century AD onwards that they appear in sharper outline – major figures are named as 'kings' or even a 'queen' and seemingly powerful confederacies emerge which the Roman state had seriously to engage with as allies or contend with as enemies. The impression is of nomads as minor irritants controlled initially through a combination of force and diplomatic engagement with petty chieftains. Later these nomads form more extensive groupings with chieftains strong enough to command wider authority and to be of greater significance to the imperial authorities. Ultimately, of course, much of the military control of the pre-desert areas of the Near

2. Evidence and methodologies

Structure	Date
Temple of Zeus	first phase AD 22-8
City Plan	by AD 75/6
South Theatre	dedicated AD 90/1
Oval Piazza	1st cent. AD
Cardo	conceived 2nd half 1st cent. AD
Cardo	Ionic colonnades – late 1st/early 2nd cent. AD ?
North Gate	AD 115
Arch	AD 129-30
South Gate	AD 129-30
City Wall	early 2nd cent. AD
Hippodrome	mid-2nd cent. AD
South Tetrakionion	mid-2nd cent. AD?
North Tetrapylon	c. AD 165
Macellum	2nd half of 2nd cent. AD
Temple of Artemis	monumentalized AD 150-80
Temple of Zeus	monumentalized 161-6
North Theatre	AD 162-6 of c. 800 seats
South Decumanus	colonnaded and paved c. AD 170
West Baths	c. AD 150-200
Nymphaeum	AD 191
Cardo	Corinthian capitals and widened – 2nd cent. AD
East Baths	2nd cent. AD?
North Theatre	extended AD 222-35 to c. 1600 seats
Baths of Paccus	AD 454-5; restored AD 584

Table 2.1. Dates of the principal structures at Gerasa.

East seems to have been entrusted to such chieftains as the imperial forces declined in numbers and effectiveness, and nomadic chieftains emerged who seemed capable of fielding significant and effective forces. The final generations of Roman rule in the Near East saw much of its security entrusted to the Christian Ghassanid confederacy which had a base in the Jawlan/ Golan. The culmination comes with the conquest of the entire Roman Near East by Arab Muslim forces coming out of Arabia.

Gerasa and the Decapolis

The evidence from the Near East as a whole for nomads is fragmented and often opaque. On the one hand we have the astonishing corpus of thousands of written texts produced by these same nomads in their own semitic language and strewn across the desert and pre-desert of precisely the eastern part of the region under investigation (see ch. 6.6). We can see, too, the progressive settlement of the pre-desert, and the personal names in Greek inscriptions from the villages that emerge there imply the populations are Arab and possibly settled nomads. There is considerable scope for interpreting and explaining the physical remains in this region but it can be paired with and illuminated by comparative research on nomadic societies and their relationship and interaction with imperial powers. There are caveats and opportunities, as one recent commentator noted:

> The comparative material is of value, not because one can simply read off the 6th c. from the better-documented recent past, but because it provokes questions and suggests a model for a comparatively small Bedu polity playing a significant role in the wider political world of the Near East (Whittow 1999: 220).

Comparative studies

Closest to home is the evidence from Roman North Africa. Nomads and semi-nomads there can be equally shadowy but in different ways from their counterparts in the Near East. Shaw has made first-class use of research on early modern Berber society in North Africa in his analysis of the growth of centres within such communities for periodic markets (Shaw 1979 [= 1995a I]; 1981). The broad insights offered from modern observation mesh harmoniously with the more fragmented evidence from Roman times. Further east, the UNESCO Libyan Valleys

2. Evidence and methodologies

Project focussed precisely on the pre-desert and desert of Tripolitania and, through a high quality fieldwork programme and multi-disciplinary approach, produced insights into the exploitation of seemingly unfruitful areas and their development in the Roman period (Barker et al. 1996).

Closer still but from more recent periods are the insights to be gained from Ottoman records for the Near East in general and the present study area in particular (Lewis 1987). Where they can be combined with archaeological evidence they can be highly illuminating and an invaluable reminder of the dangers of relying on a single type of evidence. There is a growing usage of these Ottoman records for Syria and Jordan. First, we can turn to a general treatment of settlement in Syria in the sixteenth century (Hütteroth and Abdulfattah 1977) which very importantly reminds Classicists that the exploitation of the Hauran was not just a feature of the Roman period or the nineteenth century but included episodes in the intervening centuries which should then be visible and definable in the archaeological record.

Next, there is the very useful study of the highlands of NWJ in the late nineteenth century where Ottoman records set out graphically the extent of farming in the region and the nomadic control and exploitation of the pre-desert immediately east of Gerasa (Mundy 1996). Rogan (1994) has surveyed the resettlement of the Ajlun and Belqa areas, in particular in the last two or three generations of Ottoman rule. We cannot make any simplistic equations here between Roman practice and that of modern times. The Ottoman state in the later nineteenth century had acquired overwhelming coercive firepower and reorganized its armies on western lines which gave them opportunities never seen before. Nevertheless, it is salutary to be reminded how complex a process of settlement can be. Rogan identifies three 'waves' of settlement. The first saw existing peasant communities hive off part of their population to found new villages for reasons of gain or because of internal strife. The second involved refugee colonists from Russia. They aggressively defended themselves against beduin depredations and traditional demands for protection money. They were confident, effective farmers, tied closely to the state and became good tax-payers. The third wave involved beduin tribes who saw villages springing up on 'their' land. Their leaders were persuaded to register title to secure their claims but then because they now paid tax on it they imported Palestinian and Egyptian share-croppers to farm it in the new but poor villages they created.

Probably the most valuable recent study, however, is that by Johns (1994). In this instance he is able to compare the findings from the ground surveys by himself and others in the Kerak area with the documentary evidence. The most illuminating result is that he cannot match peaks and troughs of settlement with the traditional belief that strong state control brought increased settlement and its weakening allowed nomadic intrusion and resulted in contraction. When one also introduces compensation for the poorly understood ceramics of the Islamic periods, he is able to show that the seeming collapse of settlement in the post-Roman centuries is probably greatly exaggerated. Moreover, he argues that the two great peaks of settlement – Roman and twentieth-century – are aberrations. The first coincides with the *withdrawal* of the state from direct military control and its transference to the Ghassanids. The second is the result, of course, of factors such as modern medicine, but also two others: the creation of nation states with borders and the capacity to rein-in and settle nomadic beduin, and the benefits modern Jordan derives from the role it plays in the international politics of a volatile region.

As the ceramics of the Islamic period become better understood and further fieldwork enlarges the database, it is likely that the interpretations offered by Johns will be modified, perhaps even overturned. For the moment, he has offered an

2. Evidence and methodologies

intelligent interpretation of periods often cast as little more than decline and impoverishment and has offered a new perspective on what has often been seen as the one of most note, what he calls 'the Byzantine boom'. As Johns observes:

> Seen from the peaks of the Byzantine or modern booms, the Islamic centuries seem to be characterized by long periods of almost catastrophic decline. Seen from the perspective of the longue durée, it is the Byzantine and modern booms that are freaks, caused by an extraordinary combination of external circumstances (Johns 1994: 30).

His suggestion that the 'Byzantine boom' was not the outcome of the actions of the state but of a local nomadic dynasty may be taken a little further in relation explicitly to the Hauran and Belqa with which I am concerned in this book. It has been noticed already that ground survey does seem to show a sharp decline in settlement of towns and villages in the last century of Byzantine rule in Syria (cf. a similar decline in the same period in Tripolitania: Barker et al. 1996: vol. 1, chs 11-12). The exception is the Southern Hauran and Belqa which seem to have 'bucked the general picture'. H. Kennedy (1992: 291-2) observes that the ruling Umayyad family lavished attention on their rural estates and owned one in the Belqa at 'Qubbash' from late Byzantine times till Abbassid confiscation. Bisheh (1987) has also reminded us that Umayyad notables as well as the ruling family acquired estates in the Belqa. Further evidence suggests that they settled beduin on unclaimed land in the interior of the country and that this may, in part, be what we are seeing in continuity of settlement in these two large areas. H. Kennedy (1992: 294) stresses – as Johns was to do a few years later (above) – that the extraordinary expansion of settlement at this time was exceptional: 'the Umayyad *qusur* were the product of peculiar and particular social and economic conditions which were not replicated at other times'. He goes on to find a motive in the limited tax base of the dynasty which forced them to maximize the income from lands they controlled and owned directly and whose produce could be employed in their dealings with the nomads who were central to their political welfare. As with Lepcis Magna, Shahba and the Hadrianic visit to Gerasa, this is documentary evidence archaeology could not hope to replace.

A few years later, in a review of Shahid (1995), Whittow proposed using 'the rich anthropological literature that discusses the place of the Bedu in the Ottoman empire, and the rise of dynastic polities and tribal states in the 19th- and early 20th-c. Arabia' (1999: 219). He approvingly cites (222) Khazanov (1994) in support of the view that nomads 'inevitably exist in a dialogue with the settled world'. The same people can be nomad or farmer or both, and may move back and forth between the statuses as their economic strategy requires. The crucial factor underlying the appearance of relatively powerful polities among the Arabs is the emergence of a militarily effective leader. He cites the example of the Rashids who seized Hail in 1836, became sedentary and were then able to transfer their new trade income to recruiting a non-Bedu military force that was external to the tribal support they might otherwise have had to rely on. In a second example, he points to the Sha'lan emirs of the Rwala who transcended their role as sheikhs in a fragmented tribal society by being more of a nuisance than others and thereby winning Ottoman subsidies which in turn enhanced their standing still further as they had greater rewards to share with their supporters. 'The obvious disadvantage of this method of government was that it constituted a strong encouragement for the Bedu to become more militarised and more politically developed' (Whittow 1999: 222).

Particularly illuminating now is the summary of nineteenth-century reports made by the British Consul in Aleppo to the

2. Evidence and methodologies

Foreign Office in London (Jabbur 1995: App. II). Beginning in 1835, these reports often refer to the actions of beduin tribes in unsettling Syria and blocking communications. Especially striking are the accounts of beduin raids up to the suburbs of Aleppo itself and the abandonment of villages and crops by peasants fleeing into the cities. At times tribesmen are at war with one another. On other occasions they are looting pilgrim caravans. Efforts to control them include payments, punitive expeditions and plans to construct towers in among the villages.

Much further afield are the nomadic societies on the fringes of imperial China. A great deal of research has been directed at them and there has been a resurgence in recent years as 'empires' has emerged as a significant theme in historical studies in general (e.g. Alcock et al. 2001). There, in a very different historical and social context, is the opportunity to explore the interaction of nomads and a great imperial power, their interdependence or hostility, the varied approaches – force, diplomacy, trade – of the empire to how to deal with a people and an environment they can neither overcome or ignore. Explaining the relationship is disputed. The more complex explanation (Di Cosmo 1994) reminds us that even without the presence and options exercised by a great empire towards a persistent nuisance, the actions of nomads might be stimulated by factors beyond anyone's control. In arid environments, modest shifts in, for example, rainfall, could result in significant stress if there was too little winter pasturage in the desert or even among the settled population with whom they might normally enjoy a symbiotic relationship every summer (see ch. 3).

Travellers' tales

Alongside this formal evidence we can add for the nineteenth century as a whole the fascinating if unquantifiable observations of western travellers. First is the insightful account of

Gerasa and the Decapolis

Gertrude Bell in *The Desert and the Sown,* reporting not only on the presence of nomads deep into the Belqa and across the Madaba Plain but revealing the rapid changes underway as improved security and active Ottoman colonization produced a vigorous re-settlement of arable lands which had often been deserted by farmers for centuries. Contemporary with Bell is the account of Robinson Lees (1895) who offers a brief but illuminating sketch of how the Ottoman authorities were controlling and policing the pre-desert through their diplomatic arrangements with beduin chieftains and the consequences for the latter as the empire introduced powerful new forces into their traditional arrangements.

> Even the great sheikh of the Rawallah, who has recently been created a pasha, no longer occupies the position he once held in the estimation of his brethren of the desert. His connection with the Government and the assistance it rendered has enabled him to avenge defeat of his tribe in 1885 by the Beni Sakr, but the latter are still looked upon as the champions of the anti-Turkish party, and respected accordingly; while the Adwan chief, Ali Diab, is little better than a police inspector. The Sultan, then, in degrading the Bedawin and lessening their numbers on the one hand, is creating in their stead settlers that will sooner or later push them further into the desert, or compel them to adopt the same means of earning their living that they themselves possess. This retrograde movement of the Bedawin ... is the course usually taken by all Governments when developing the resources of a country. It has one ill effect – it turns many into thieves and robbers that were otherwise less disposed to that form of annoyance; but it also furnishes the Government with a further excuse for weakening their power, in its efforts to capture and punish offenders. Where a few years ago these people lived in

2. Evidence and methodologies

contentment ... we find them full of complaint – of the soldiers, Circassians, and Government. They cling more tenaciously to their land, and resist by force any encroachment; but they are on the losing side, and before long the progress of events across the Jordan will have developed so far as to dispossess the present lords of the soil, and place in their stead a people not only more industrious, but more religious, and more inclined to pay the taxes. The change that is now going on over the Jordan will develop the natural resources of the provinces occupied by the new settlers, but whether it will yield a corresponding degree of peace and happiness remains to be seen (Lees 1895: 6-7).

*

In the Roman Near East, the imperial authorities, too, must often have engaged in initiatives to deal with a people who were – in their view – a part of their *imperium* but whose way of life, mobility and independence made them difficult to control in the way they could with settled farming communities. As one recent commentator observes, the beduin were not a major threat; they were, however, a 'dangerous nuisance; but to ignore or defy them tended to be costly and futile...' (Whittow 1999: 222). One possible method of control may be what we see in the archaeological record: the imperial penetration of the pre-desert and desert with roads and garrisons and the enticement of significant numbers of nomads into farming communities in previously unsettled areas (ch. 4). But the other examples summarised here remind us that the obvious explanation generally favoured, is not the only possibility or necessarily the best.

3

The natural and human landscape and environment

Within the generally higher level of development encouraged by Roman imperialism, however, there were clear opportunities for what I would call hot spots of development that were made possible by combining regional peculiarities with highly centralized Mediterranean-wide systems of connectivity. In this case, as Horden and Purcell eloquently argue, it is nonsensical to speak of intrinsic characteristics of any given micro-region of the Mediterranean: considered in isolation, such regions might appear quite unpromising, but when connected, they can suddenly flourish.

Shaw 2001b: 432

3.1. Introduction

The region can be viewed in three ways (ch. 3.3). At the core is a micro-region in NWJ, the Highlands of Ajlun. It is a discrete area of highlands, characterised by rich soils, abundant rainfall and an impressive scatter of urban centres originating in the Bronze Age but most notable in the LCM when several of the cities of the Decapolis lay here. Second, there is the Jordan River valley to the west, then the immediately surrounding micro-regions of hill and plain to the south (al-Belqa), and steppe and desert to the east. Finally, this group of micro-regions is itself collectively a discrete unit, a 'virtual island',

3. The natural and human landscape and environment

isolated by geography and to some extent by environment from the wider world both of the Mediterranean and of the Syrian and Arabian Deserts. As such it looks west as we might expect and was part of the Mediterranean world. But it looked east, too, and was part of this immense desert world stretching off to the Gulf.

In broad structural terms the region has been unchanged throughout the Holocene. Defining its geographical character – landform – is simple and provides an invaluable preliminary framework for explaining and interpreting its settlement history. Soils are more difficult. There is no reason to doubt that the broad map of their types and location is fundamentally unchanged since the start of the Holocene but little can be said at the moment about erosion. Only recently has systematic work begun on soil history in this part of Jordan and the results are very tentative. Exploration of the land around Abila led to the provisional conclusion that there was little evidence of erosion of the red soils, the material found in wadi bottoms seemingly having eroded out of the substrata rather than the surface soils. On the other hand, the character of the soils, relatively shallow and rich in calcium carbonate, has been seen as a weakness if climate altered and precipitation declined. Agriculture then would be vulnerable to lower yields (Lucke et al. 2005).

Much more problematic is defining the environment during the LCM – rainfall patterns are crucial. Recent studies have begun to illuminate the question of ancient environments in this region and in a highly suggestive way. Research is uneven and some is in a very early stage, but there are exciting and significant developments which can already be integrated into the study of the human geography of the region. After decades of privileging anthropogenic explanations for the character of ancient cultures and for change, archaeologists are again accepting that geography and environment may have played a more significant role than it has been fashionable to allow for half a century (below).

3.2. A 'virtual island'

Horden and Purcell have redefined the Mediterranean world for us in terms of connected micro-regions and many have found this a far more satisfying vision than the overall unity Braudel proposed but which seemed hard to reconcile with the diversity he simultaneously proclaimed. Micro-regions individually may often be poor supporters of human settlement especially in the frequently unfavourable conditions of the Mediterranean. Their very poverty, however, can be a stimulant to ingenuity, and micro-regions may collectively amount to far more than the sum of their parts. Instead of small-scale and limited mixed farming everywhere, regions can develop through increased and widespread specialization and exchange. Within the context of still greater units – states or empires – the degree of specialization can be pursued further and the potential of specific regions to produce principally grain or olive oil or wool or timber... can be developed extensively. The key term here is 'connectivity' (Horden and Purcell 2000: ch. V; cf. Shaw 2001b). The concept is an attractive one and can be applied successfully to NWJ (below).

However, Horden and Purcell introduce a further concept – some micro-regions or groups of micro-regions may be seen as distinctive because of their extreme isolation. In such cases one confronts what the authors describe as a 'virtual island' (2000: 65). Their example is Cyrenaica (2000: 65-74; cf. Shaw 2006: 3 for further 'virtual islands' in the northwestern part of North Africa). Although there are communications on all sides, Cyrenaica is a stubby peninsula, sea or deep desert isolating it on all sides. The term 'virtual island' does not, of course, require total isolation. Indeed, in the case of Cyrenaica it was a region made prosperous by its export of large olive oil surpluses and,

3. The natural and human landscape and environment

very curiously, it was only one part of a Roman province, the other half of which was the distant island of Crete. But it was isolated in significant ways and introverted and these became during the Roman centuries in particular, vital features in explaining the dynamics of development and the distinctive culture to emerge there.

From the Highlands of Ajlun in NWJ, the Mediterranean can be as little as 60 km away, visible on a clear day. It might seem no more than a journey of two or three days on foot and the viewer could certainly feel very much a part of the world surrounded by the great sea and its hinterlands. But in between, plunging to below minus 200 m, lies the deep trough of the Jordan Valley. In a world where distance was more realistically measured in time than miles, the sea and coastal plain were in fact several days away and would involve considerable exertion.

The Jordan River is fed by a succession of streams and rivers joining it from west and east and all flowing parallel to one another (Fig. 3.1). Most are modest, no serious impediment to travellers. But there are two major exceptions. In the north the Wadi Yarmuk begins as a network of tributaries north and south of Adraha/ Deraa, c. 40 km to the east of the Jordan Valley. The Yarmuk itself and the deep and sinuous course of the Wadi ash-Shallalah joining it from the southeast are notable impediments to movement. They all converge and soon slice into the landscape to run through a deeply incised valley where the stream is some 400 m below the plateau on either side. Finally it enters the Jordan just below the Sea of Galilee.

As one travels south from the Highlands of Ajlun, the route is barred by the winding course of the River Zarqa. The river in this case is a significant one, rising near Amman then running north then west to join the Jordan. It presents an impressive view but it does not in fact seriously impede communications on the various north-south routes between the highlands to the north and the hills and plain to south. Beyond the plain, how-

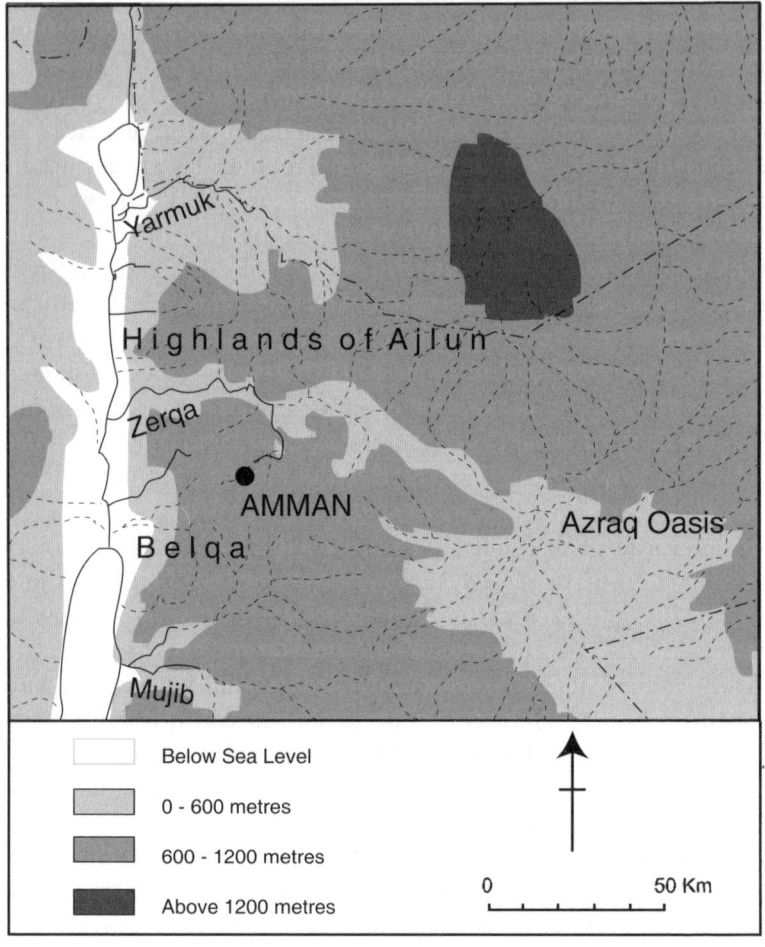

Fig. 3.1. Physical geography of Northwest Jordan.

ever, the traveller does encounter major natural obstacles in the form of first the Wadi Wala, then the much more daunting Wadi Mujib. Both lead into the Dead Sea and are the result of perennial streams which have cut their way deep into the plateau which stretches south from near Amman. The plateau

3. The natural and human landscape and environment

continues beyond these great slashes in the landscape but the wadis, especially the Mujib, create a significant barrier to easy movement. Even today, when a surfaced and well-engineered road crosses the canyon and motorized transport carries the burden, little traffic does in fact cross from one side to the other. Communities on either side are only 5 km apart but the deep plunge and tortuous route discourage most movement.

The fourth side of this 'virtual island' is the desert to the east. In practice, the highlands in the northwest and the plateau in the south stretch eastwards, becoming progressively more arid and lower in elevation. Vegetation becomes sparser and soils are poorer. Finally, one is in desert: soils are very poor, precipitation is negligible and vegetation is little more than camel thorn or modest bushes and trees along seasonal wadis. Wadis can be impressive torrents in winter but are dry for much of the summer and there are few places where pools or springs can be found or even the scope for digging wells to tap into ground water. The desert stretches eastwards into Syria, Iraq and Saudi Arabia forming a deep barrier.

The 'island' is, of course, accessible and there are communications with the wider region on all sides. People did cross the Jordan/ Dead Sea, the Yarmuk and Mujib, while nomads moved seasonally between summer pasturage in the west and winter in the desert and traders from Arabia and as far away as the Gulf moved back and forth. Nevertheless, the inhabitants of the region as a whole will have been more introverted than the inhabitants of the Mediterranean coastal belt or those of the interior of Syria. What that may or did mean in practice will be returned to in the final section.

3.3. Broad patterns

The 'island' is large, stretching from the Jordan Valley and Dead Sea to the Azraq Basin; from the Southern Hauran to the

Gerasa and the Decapolis

Wadi Mujib: a quadrilateral *c.* 150 km wide by *c.* 150 km deep, about 22,500 sq km.

The region can be broken down into five units or microregions (Fig. 3.2). On the west side is the broad, deep trough of the **Jordan Valley (1).** In the northwest are the **Ajlun Highlands (2)**. To the south lies the **Belqa (3)**, a distinctive region of broad plains. To the east of the highlands lies the **pre-desert (4).** And beyond that the **desert (5)** to and far beyond the Azraq Oasis. Some of these can be sub-divided into discrete sub-units (cf. ch. 3.4). The rift valley comprises both the rich alluvial plain of the River Jordan and the arid landscape along the eastern shore of the Dead Sea fed by a few springs and streams, the 'wilderness' around the Arnon (Wadi Mujib) favoured by ascetic

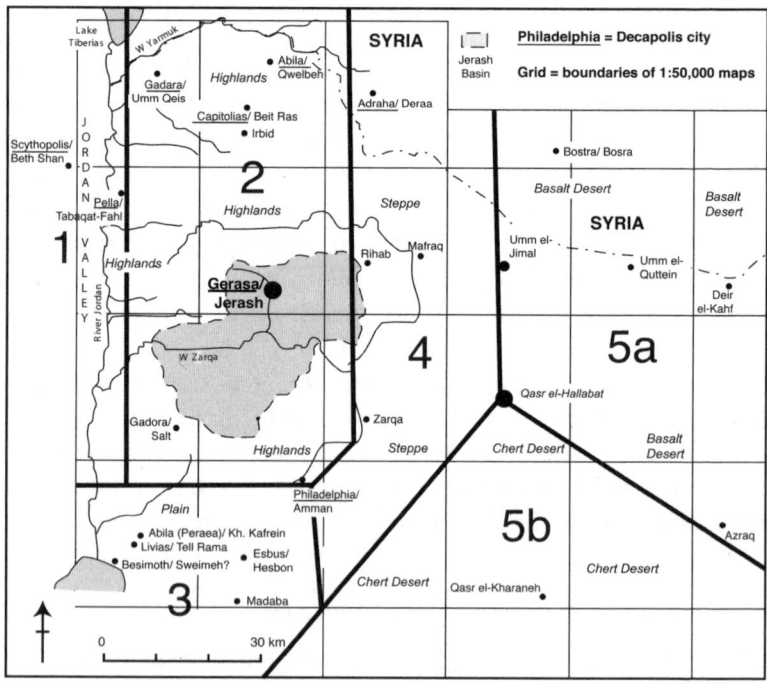

Fig. 3.2. The micro-regions of Northwest Jordan.

3. The natural and human landscape and environment

monks in late Roman times. The Belqa consists of hilly upland country in the north – Amman/ Philadelphia is, surprisingly, 300 m higher in elevation than Gerasa and 500 m higher than Gadara. In the south, however, it gives way to the broad expanse of the Madaba Plain (Fig. 3.3). The pre-desert comprises the relatively narrow belt of land east of Jiza, Amman and Zarqa but then the great eastwards out-thrust of the Southern Hauran intruding into the Basalt Desert. The desert is of two types – the Basalt Desert of the north and the Chert Desert to its south. Within the former higher rainfall and richer soils differentiate the northern part from the arid south.

The broad character of the entire region can be presented simply through a series of maps. Fig. 3.2 displays the physical geography emphasizing the significance of the highland area from Gadara to Philadelphia as the area of intense urban development. In an arc around it from Madaba to Bostra are the secondary urban centres, developed after those of the Decapolis. Beyond that again, the belt of pre-desert where military sites, villages and farms abound. Finally there are the deserts and Qasr el-Hallabat. The latter lies at the juncture of the Chert and Basalt Deserts and where they in turn meet the pre-desert. The same figure displays graphically the drainage westwards into the Jordan Valley and Dead Sea to the west and into the Azraq Basin to the east. In broad terms, after rising steeply from the Jordan Valley, the land slopes off southeast to Azraq and to the great trough of the Azraq-Sirhan Depression.

Fig. 3.4a displays the recent rainfall pattern. Of course it represents an average over a number of years and obscures the great deal of local variety as well as the inter-annual variability in patterns. One can see that there is normally abundant rainfall in the Ajlun Highlands and the northern Belqa for crops of all kinds. Moreover, there is often adequate rainfall over much of the northern Madaba Plain and parts of the pre-desert to support cereals, certainly barley. Farmers normally need to

Fig. 3.3. Aerial view of the Madaba Plain at Esbus (Hisban) (APA02/ 33.32; 2 October 2002).

3. The natural and human landscape and environment

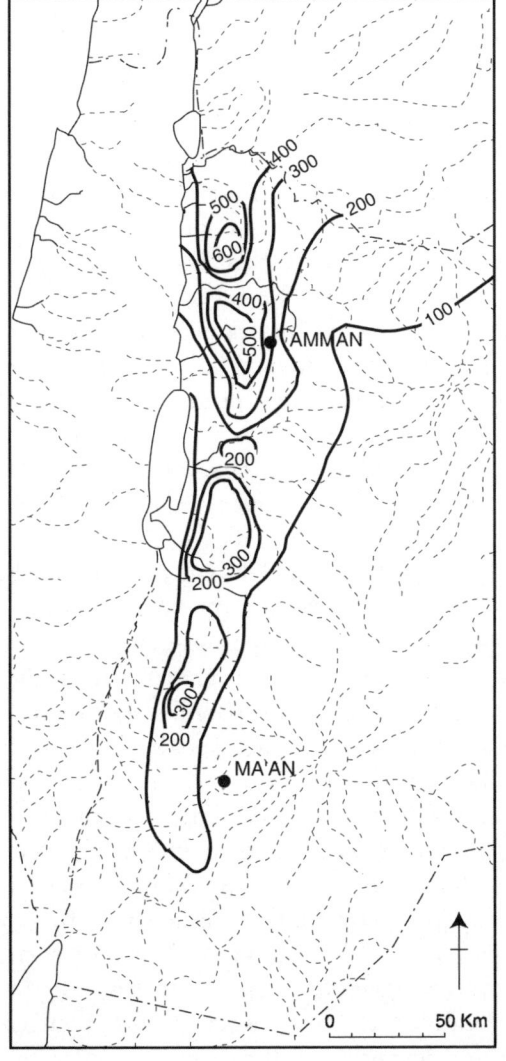

Fig. 3.4a. Rainfall pattern (from Kennedy 2004b: 32).

rely on a minimum of 200 mm of rainfall to grow wheat but barley will grow with less than that. In this case the isohyet suggests that cereals – the thirstiest of the potential crops – can be grown widely across three of the micro-regions.

Precipitation is the most significant source of water for farmers, but in this instance there are two other sources. The Jordan itself offered a perennial source of water between the Sea of Galilee and the Dead Sea, farmers using its waters to irrigate the valley's rich alluvial soils and grow the thirsty vegetables and fruits which it still produces. Second is the great oasis at Azraq, the second largest (after Palmyra) in the Syrian Desert. Until recent excessive pumping emptied them, there were two perennial lakes at Azraq, and the supply there which had flowed underground from the volcanic Ledja in southern Syria, offered immense reserves of fresh water. There are also numerous places in the highlands and Belqa where much more modest springs are found which can provide local supplies in addition to rainfall and those can be important in creating internal diversity within the micro-regions.

Fig. 3.4b looks at the same region for its soils and it is a surprisingly optimistic picture (Bender 1974: ch. 7). The rich alluvial soils of the Jordan Valley speak for themselves, carried down from the surrounding more vegetated slopes and enriched by occasional flooding. The Red Mediterranean Soils are by far the richest, capable of supporting a wide range of crops including grapes, olives, nuts and stone-fruits. As the map shows, these soils are spread over a wide area, coinciding broadly with the higher rainfall of the region. Yellow Mediterranean Soils are attractive for agriculture, too, but are less rich and their spread is broadly in the area of pre-desert/ Southern Hauran. Poorer soil and lower rainfall can still support barley by dry farming, local irrigation will support thirstier garden crops and in general the land is suited to grazing. The Southern Hauran is especially striking as a pocket of both higher rainfall thrust

3. The natural and human landscape and environment

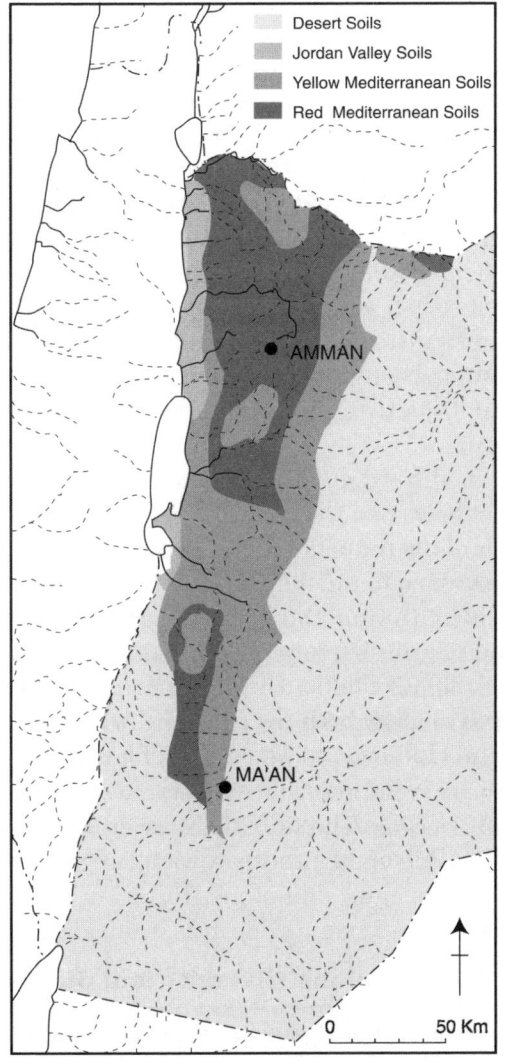

Fig. 3.4b. Soils (from Kennedy 2004b: 32).

out to the east and of richer soils. As we shall see, it is a distinctive area of arable farming and one of the barometers of settlement in the region. Finally, almost one third of the region is Desert Soils with limited nutrients and they are in an area of minimal rainfall. But the desert is of two kinds. The Chert Desert in the south has little vegetation beyond what is visible along the seasonal water courses (wadis). The Basalt Desert, whose surface is extensively strewn with the basalt boulders that are the product of volcanic activity in southern Syria (the Jabal Druze) spewing out molten droplets, looks forbidding. In practice, it supports more vegetation than the Chert Desert as is reflected in the greater concentration of evidence for human activity there.

Figs 3.5a and b set out the evidence for the distribution of natural vegetation and the agricultural areas. The two significant features of the natural vegetation map are the distribution of the 'Mediterranean scrub' which includes tree cover (mainly oak) throughout the highlands and northern Belqa, and the broad spread of grasslands with, once again, a projection eastwards to encompass the Southern Hauran. The two crop maps (Figs 3.6a and b) show both the spread of wheat growing where the highest precipitation is found and of barley eastwards into areas where there is too little rainfall for wheat. Olives and grapes are supported in broadly the same area of the highlands and Belqa but olives are more concentrated on the eastern slopes of the hills.

3.4. Micro-regions: diversity and difference

The principal concept of Horden and Purcell's re-interpretation of the Mediterranean world is that one should view it as a patchwork of micro-regions. These are highly varied in size and character. They are not necessarily internally homogenous – indeed, they are often (as with the Biqa Valley in Lebanon:

3. The natural and human landscape and environment

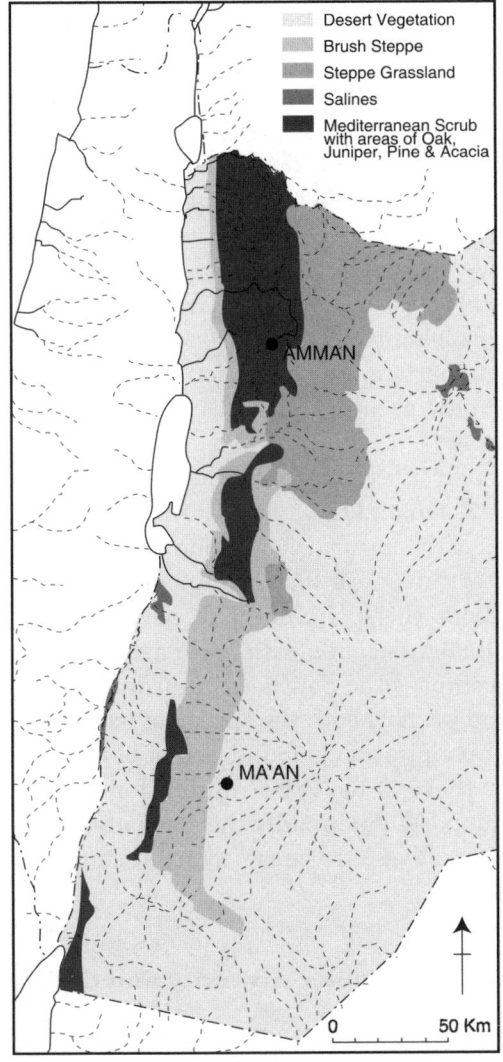

Fig. 3.5a. Natural vegetation (from Kennedy 2004b: 33).

Gerasa and the Decapolis

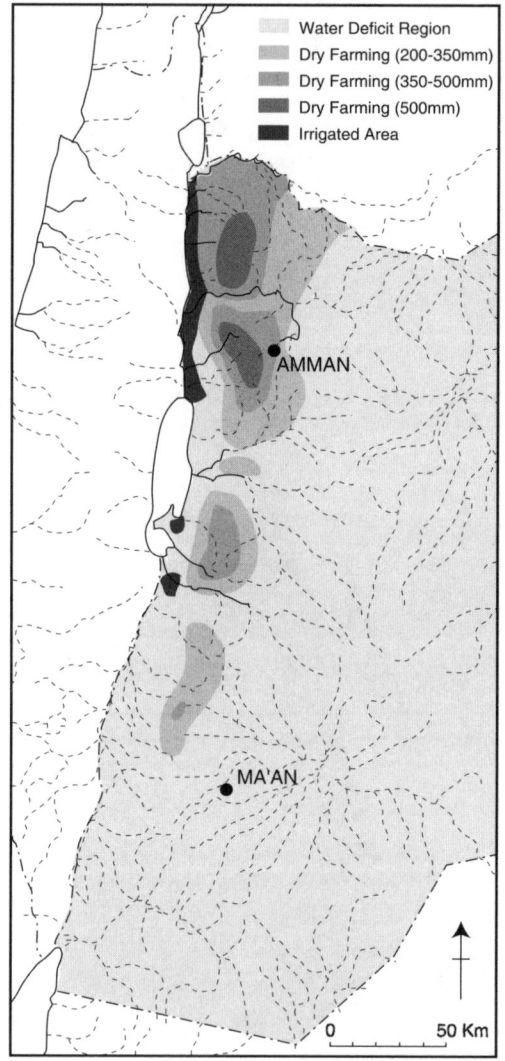

Fig. 3.5b. Agricultural areas (from Kennedy 2004b: 33).

3. The natural and human landscape and environment

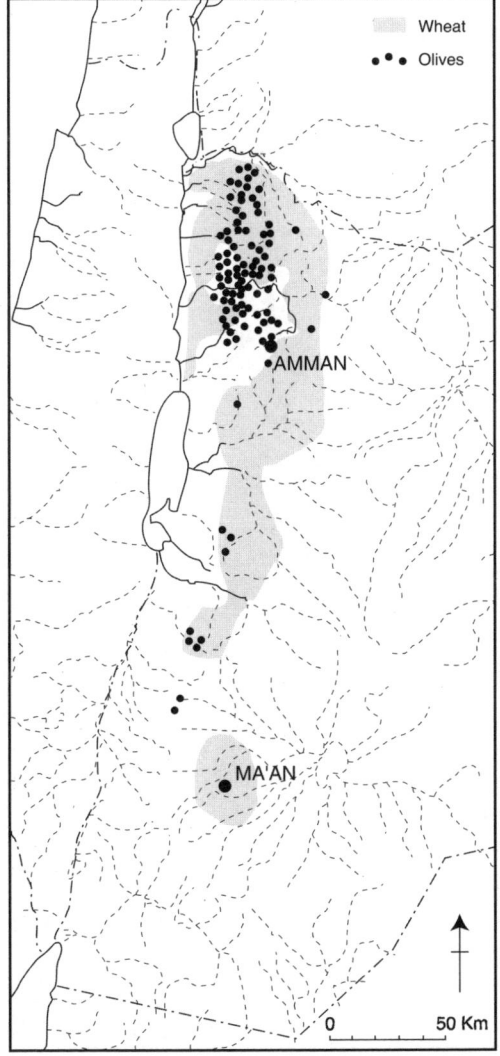

Fig. 3.6a. Planted areas for wheat and olives (from Kennedy 2004b: 34).

Gerasa and the Decapolis

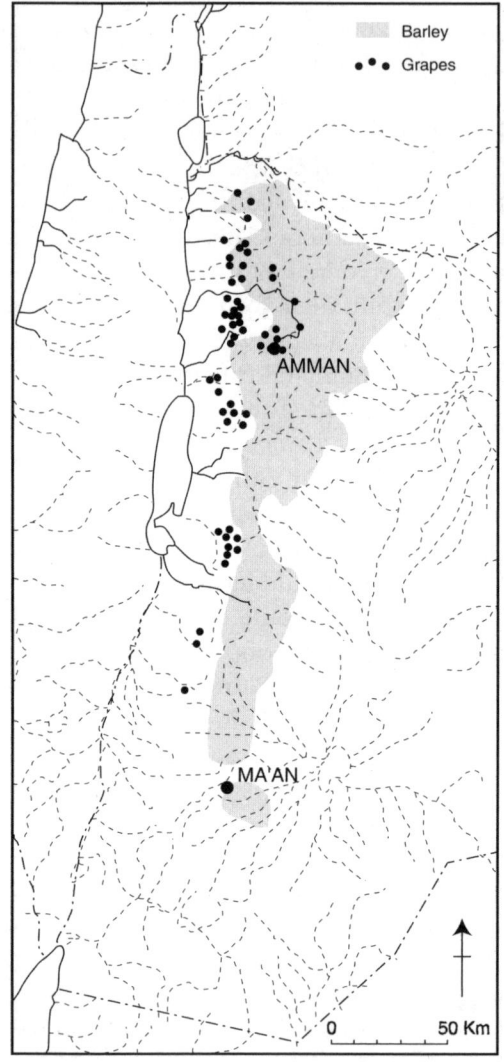

Fig. 3.6b. Planted areas for barley and grapes (from Kennedy 2004b: 34).

3. The natural and human landscape and environment

Horden and Purcell 2000: 54-9) very varied internally as well. Indeed, it is the variability and the consequences of adjusting to that which gives Mediterranean societies their distinctive character. But Horden and Purcell go further and argue, very convincingly, that many of the micro-regions of the Mediterranean achieve prosperity and significance only when they interact – 'connect' – with others. The limitations to growth and development are overcome when the inhabitants of a micro-region are able to shift their focus from a broadly-based and diverse food-production strategy to specialization. As we shall see, there is much to commend this interpretation as an explanation for the development of this region.

The maps tell the broad story of what is possible and where. As we have seen, the Jordan Valley supports intensive cultivation of all kinds of crops but is especially suited to garden-type cultivation of vegetables and fruits that require plenty of water. Pre-industrial transport would have severely limited the scope for cash-cropping and we should certainly envisage the valley being used also for the cultivation of cereals and tree crops. On the other hand, the nature of the valley and its reliance on irrigation rather then rainfall meant that it was far more uniform than the other micro-regions.

A first point to make about all the other micro-regions is that the rainfall pattern presented in the map above is misleading. What is striking about so much of the Mediterranean world as a whole is that there can be enormous differences in rainfall from year to year. Hence the proverb, 'The year bears the crop not the soil' (cited in Osborne 1987: 31). Where the average rainfall is high as in much of the highlands and parts of the Belqa, this inter-annual variability might have limited effects on crops. Even the lowest level was perfectly adequate for all the crops grown. But further south and east where rainfall was lower, inter-annual variability in rainfall mattered very much. Farmers cannot plant crops on the basis of *average* rainfall but in the knowledge of the *reliable* minimum likely. In short, in areas where wheat *could* be grown in some years, farmers would be wiser nevertheless to plan for the possibility of inadequate rainfall and plant barley instead (Lucke et al. forthcoming).

Further east still where even the rainfall for growing barley might not be enough, one was more likely to encounter nomads or semi-nomads. Their survival strategy was more varied and they could, therefore, sow seed opportunistically. Even in recent times it was not unusual for beduin in similar areas in the Negev Desert to carry out crude soil preparation, sow seed then depart for winter pasturage leaving the fields with no further maintenance until their seasonal return months later. Their livelihood was not dependent on a favourable outcome. In these eastern areas the opportunity for cropping was more limited in its extent. Suitable soils were not just thinner but came in pockets. The margins of seasonal water courses are one obvious location and these are almost invariably to be found in the Basalt Desert and most notably around the fringes of the Southern Hauran. As we shall see, these often involved simple water-impeding structures which created small fields. Although they are less common and extensive, they follow a very similar pattern to the well-known examples in the Negev Desert (Evenari et al. 1982; Kennedy 1998a).

But let us return now to a closer exploration of the core micro-region, the Ajlun Highlands (Fig. 3.7). Here one can see to good effect the enormous internal variability just by looking at the environments of some of the Decapolis cities. Gerasa is the best-known of these. There one finds a wide basin in which the city lies. Soils are rich in the immediate vicinity of the city, especially along the course of the perennial Wadi Jarash. There, in addition to direct watering from precipitation, there is evidence for channels tapping water upstream and conducting it by a shallower gradient to water the soils on either bank

3. The natural and human landscape and environment

Fig. 3.7. Aerial view of the Jarash Basin (APA98/ 25.24; 17 May 1998).

downstream. There is no direct evidence for tillage inside the town itself but there is a growing body of evidence for gardens inside Roman towns. Above the ancient town is a succession of springs in the outcrops above the Wadi Jarash from which water could be led down onto garden-like fields. Within a short distance of Gerasa itself, farmers practised rainfall and irrigation farming. Although we cannot define the nature of farming at Gerasa in the Roman period, we might legitimately infer a mixture of garden-like cultivation in and close to the town itself; further afield, as today, cultivation would involve cereals (wheat) interspersed with vines and olives. Although there are rich soils in the basin around Jarash, there are also extensive areas of rocky outcrops. As one begins to rise up the surrounding slopes fields become rockier and narrower as they fit into pockets of soil beside minor gullies. In short, despite the glowing picture suggested by the soil and rainfall maps, the quality of cultivable land could be very varied. We cannot in this instance define how land was actually shared, or if farmers cultivated several small parcels of different kinds of soil and suitability as a risk-management strategy. Overall, however, that would be the effect. The basic food supply of Gerasa would be provided by gardens, rich cereal fields, smaller rocky hillside fields and terraced 'fields' higher still. In addition, we need to factor in livestock. Some would be the animals of the farmers – probably mainly goats/ sheep as today, but also chickens, perhaps pigs and even some cattle needed for traction if not for milk or meat. But there would also be the seasonally available livestock. Nomads and farmers, at their most harmonious, enjoyed a symbiotic relationship. Seasonally, nomads supplied extra manpower at harvest time, their camels could assist with transport and ploughing while their goats and sheep could graze on stubble while simultaneously manuring the land. Surplus meat and dairy products, hides and leather products could be exchanged for grain and tools.

3. The natural and human landscape and environment

A similar variability is found around other Decapolis cities. Gadara is perched on a high ridge – there is no stream of any kind and water was brought to the city by elaborate tunnels from some 20 km away. Rich soils cover the slopes falling away on all sides. Today they are thickly populated with thousands of olive trees between which cereals are often sown. Philadelphia does have a perennial stream – the Wadi Amman is in fact the start of what becomes the Wadi Zarqa. The soils are as rich as elsewhere in the Decapolis but rainfall is lower. Indeed, Philadelphia lies on a high plateau close to the edge of the pre-desert and at this point the latter is a very narrow belt. As others have observed, it feels more arid and the proximity of the desert is palpable. The hinterland is again a mixture of moderately sized rich plains and pockets of good soils interspersed with rock outcropping. Terracing would have been more restricted to the steep-sided valleys in the immediate vicinity of the town rather than further away where the land was flatter. As always, water was a key element and something of the nature of the precipitation may be gauged from the reputation of Philadelphia in antiquity as a centre for horse-breeding. Indeed, the grasslands of the pre-desert on the immediate east of the city would have seemed ideal for grazing.

The other micro-regions are also varied internally but to a lesser extent. Within the Belqa, as the name implies, the Madaba Plain offers an extensive area of generally flat landscape with excellent scope for cereal cultivation very much perhaps as it appears today. It is marked by two cities in the Roman period, Esbus and Madaba.

To the east, the pre-desert lands were equally suited for cereals. The first region encountered is that stretching from just east of Gerasa as far almost as Qasr el-Hallabat. Its principal place is Rihab which lies at the centre of what may be defined as the Rihab Plain. It is a region in which wheat can be grown annually although barley might be safer on the eastern fringe. The numerous ruins of ancient villages (ch. 4.4) underscore the extent to which it could be and was settled in antiquity.

Beyond, to the northeast again, one enters the strange landscape of the Southern Hauran. The black basalt boulders that cover so much of it and from which field walls, animal pens, animal traps, towers, forts and houses are built are forbidding. But the region is in fact relatively well-watered from rainfall and suited to barley growing. Beneath almost every modern beduin village are the remains of a predecessor, giving scores of ruined ancient villages of, broadly, the LCM. They are well-built and testimony to the strength of the local economy with quite extensive stands of olives and, closer to the settlements, gardens of plants requiring more regular watering.

This last brings us to a feature of the region which is crucial in explaining the success of farming. Rainfall is seasonal and increasingly slight as one moves further east. But the peoples of the much wider region from North Africa through the Middle East had long before – certainly since the Bronze Age – developed technologies to harvest and store water for the dry months of the year. Two of these have already been alluded to in this chapter. First is a simple device for impeding water and retaining moisture. Low walls, often no more than a mounding of field boulders, are set out across the direction of flow of shallow seasonal wadis. These cross-wadi walls have a two-fold effect. First, the walls cause water rushing down the wadi to slow and pond behind each wall before finally flowing over the top and heading on to pond behind the next wall just a few metres downstream. Sediments in the water settle during the ponding process and gradually 'soil' builds up in what are then small fields trailing back in a triangular shape behind each wall. Once these 'fields' are formed, ponding also penetrates and soaks into the deep soils where some is retained for the crops (barley) sown. There are some excellent examples in the pre-desert

3. The natural and human landscape and environment

Fig. 3.8. Photo of cross-walls in Northwest Jordan (APA02.1/ SL7.29; 1 April 2002).

between Qasr el-Hallabat and Umm el-Jimal in the Southern Hauran (Fig. 3.8) (Kennedy 1998a: 67-73; Kennedy and Bewley 2004: 39, Fig. 2.12).

Second, here and there one finds traces of channels tapping water off a seasonal water-course, conducting it by a gentler gradient to a point downstream where it can either be used to irrigate a pocket of valley soils or, more commonly, to fill an open reservoir for storage. Great reservoirs abound in the region from the Madaba Plain to the eastern extreme of the Southern Hauran. The largest, at Jiza on the eastern edge of the Madaba Plain where the pre-desert begins, could hold up to c. 68,000 cubic metres of water and is often still used for watering large flocks. Third, and by far the most common, are the cisterns (Fig. 3.9). These are found in huge numbers throughout the entire region but are especially common in those parts where rainfall had to be harvested and stored. Although they date in some cases as far back as before 3000 BC,

Gerasa and the Decapolis

Fig. 3.9. Cistern in Umm el-Quttein.

they continued to be constructed in every period. In short, in the pre-desert and Southern Hauran. Fig. 3.10 illustrates the extent to which these are found: an astonishing 1431 cisterns and 39 large reservoirs. We should not underestimate their significance. Wahlin (1997) has stressed their numbers and immense combined capacity and that their water was regarded as sweet and largely for human consumption.

3.5. Natural routes

In the west of the region the water courses, whether dry or perennial, run in a east-west direction, their valleys suggesting the easiest direction for movement. On the east, however, they drain eastwards into the Azraq Depression. One part of the eastern region is distinctive, however. From the Azraq Oasis itself, stretching northwestwards, is a series of broad areas of mudpan which become shallow but extensive seasonal lakes

3. The natural and human landscape and environment

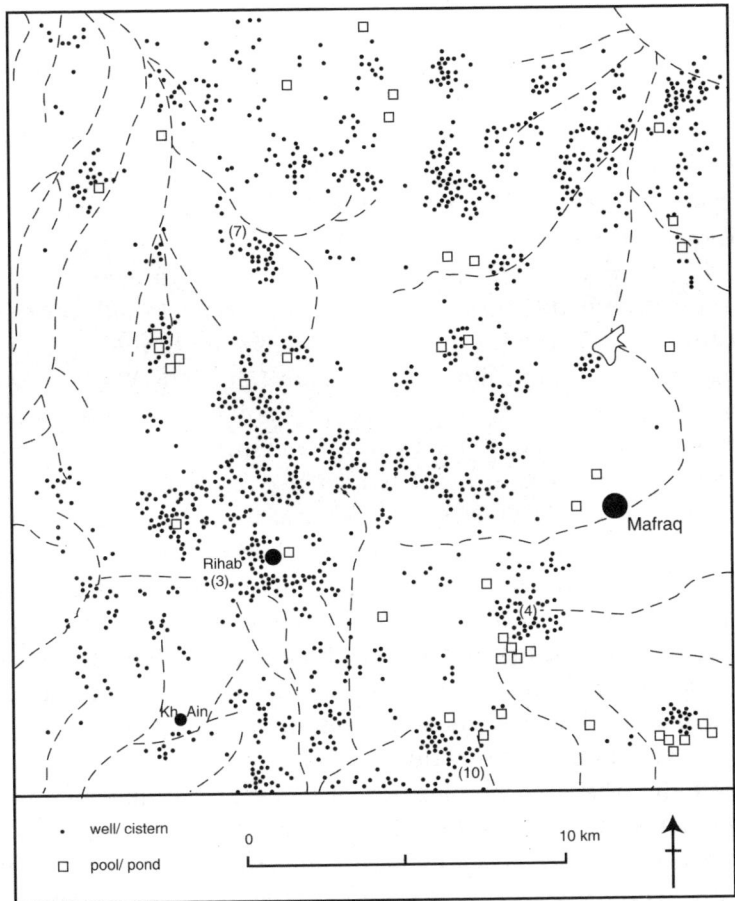

Fig. 3.10. The sheet of the 1:50,000 series covers an area of c. 650 km². The map conventions record as 'wells' what are in fact covered cisterns and, of course, it is recording only those visible to the mapper who was working from air photographs and interpreting – probably always correctly – the tiny black dots visible on the 1953 photographs as the shadow inside the open void of a cistern whose roof has collapsed. Some will certainly be misidentified; on the other hand those still roofed, or now filled in or otherwise hidden will be unrecorded. The exercise is illustrative of the enormous numbers still in existence in and around what are settlements of, principally, the LCM. The bunching reflects the location of settlements.

after rain. As mapped (see Fig. 4.2) they suggest a natural route along a broad depression which seasonally held water, from the oasis to the nodal point of Qasr el-Hallabat from which routes ran west into the Decapolis or north (by a recently confirmed Roman road) to the small Nabataean-Roman-Umayyad town of Umm el-Jimal and the nearby Roman highway, the *Via Nova Traiana* (Kennedy 1997b).

In contrast, the strategic highways of the ancient world largely ran north-south (Fig. 4.2). The section of the *Via Nova Traiana* completed in AD 114 which ran from Philadelphia to Bostra was able to follow the first stretch of the Wadi Zarqa then to strike off across low hills then the relatively flat pre-desert without serious engineering challenges. The King's Highway in contrast had to rise and fall as it crossed a succession of east-west water courses and hills then highlands as it ran north from Philadelphia through Gerasa. Other Roman roads followed more mixed routes. That from Gadara to Bostra, for example, was partly following the grain of the Wadi Yarmuk but in fact had to constantly cross its tributaries including some such as the Wadi esh-Shallalah which offered a serious impediment and required a two-storeyed bridge at one point.

Finally, there is the question of crossing the River Jordan (Roll 2002). Today it is a muddy stream, the outcome of water drawn off its tributaries for irrigation. In earlier centuries it was a significant river. There were at least four major highways that had to negotiate it: between Gadara and Tiberias, Pella and Scythopolis, Philadelphia and Neapolis and Esbus and Jericho. In the early nineteenth century travellers reported a ten-arched bridge on the first of these (Irby and Mangles 1823 [1844]: 90-1) and another was visible on the third. Further evidence is on the Madaba Mosaic map where there appear to be two places with frameworks across the river for hauling a ferry across (Piccirillo 1993: 28, 62 and 94). Strabo (*Geog.*

3. The natural and human landscape and environment

16.2.16) reports that the Jordan was navigable and certainly the Dead Sea was used for shipping.

3.6. Ancient climate and environment

The detailed survey above (ch. 3.4) largely glosses over a central problem: to what extent is the *modern* climate relevant to the ancient world? In particular, was the ancient climate significantly different from today's? This is a crucial question for much of a region that is agriculturally marginal. Even modest differences in precipitation can be pivotal in determining whether the pre-desert in particular can be used for cereal cultivation and settlement and the extent to which thirsty crops can be grown even in the highlands.

Two aspects of this question must be addressed. First, to what extent can we reconstruct the climate of the first millennia BC and AD? Second, to what extent is the archaeological record for that period determined by the climate?

During the last century views polarized twice on the question of climatic determinism as a driving force in explaining historical processes and events, and we are now moving towards some kind of equilibrium (Issar and Zohar 2004: ch. 1). Ellsworth Huntingdon launched the first assault in relation to the Middle East with what came to be known as Huntington's Deterministic School which argued that geography (including climate) moulded what any given region might support and determined the character of the society (Huntington 1924). By mid-century there had been a reaction and archaeologists were convinced that human agency – anthropogenic factors – were crucial. Humankind was not helplessly at the mercy of geography and environment but could respond, circumvent and master them. Indeed, it might be precisely the struggle to overcome the inadequacies of one's environment that would produce great leaps forward. In the last generation there has been a great deal of work done on climate in particular and there is again a willingness to see detectable major fluctuations as affecting human societies significantly. This is not a return to uncritical determinism but rather an acceptance that the factors driving the development or collapse of cultures are numerous and varied. That, of course, raises an important question: among a variety of factors, as they are not all of equal importance, is there any one that is dominant? The most recent survey and interpretation of climatic evidence is clear that climatic change is the dominant force (Issar and Zohar 2004: ch. 2).

Written sources for ancient climate may offer anecdotal evidence for conditions or changes but they are imprecise and generally worthless (Rubin 1989: 74-5 citing vague references to conditions – 'waterless', 'desert'). Instead one must turn to the sciences for conditions in earlier times. There are various types of proxy data. First, climate is reflected in the flora of a given region. Finding and analysing ancient pollen reveals the range of species growing locally and the balance between them. Detailed knowledge of the species indicates the nature of the climate: wet, humid, cold, warm etc. Second, there is the evidence of tree-rings reflecting the type of growing season year by year. Third is the evidence of shorelines of lakes or seas, sand dunes far inland which reveal higher sea levels in the past or the annual deposition of sediments in what are known as terminal lakes. Hand in hand with this kind of research must go that of dating. A sequence of relative dates may be useful but for present purposes and for most archaeological research, absolute dates are vital. Fortunately, there is a growing body of such dates and a growing confidence in setting out at least the broad chronology of what seems to have been a significant shift in climate during the LCL.

First, there is the suggestive evidence from an unexpected source: the trunks of tamarisk trees incorporated into the Roman siege-ramp at Masada and dated, therefore, to felling in or

3. The natural and human landscape and environment

around AD 70 precisely. Acacia and tamarisk trees are common in the vicinity today and their balance in the landscape reflects the contemporary moisture levels. In the case of those at Masada, the balance is firmly in favour of tamarisk, implying moister conditions, and is different from the pattern around there today which favours more acacia in contemporary arid conditions (Issar and Zohar 2004: 30-2).

Tree-rings can be a wonderful source not just of absolute dates but as a proxy for ancient climates. Recent work on tree-rings from Jordan has pointed the way to what may one day be achieved there but at the moment the sequence for northern Jordan goes back only a century while even that for southern Jordan is limited to the period 1600-1995 (Touchan and Hughes 1999). However, more recently, in a brief report, Lucke et al. (forthcoming) have announced investigation of trees in NWJ with ages of 200-450+ years. Plainly the potential exists.

Much more useful is the work done on the large bodies of water in the wider region. Israeli scientists recently extracted a core from the bed of the Sea of Galilee. The layers preserve the depositional history of sediment carried into the lake annually including pollen from the flora growing within the lake's catchment area (Stiller et al. 1983-4; Issar and Zohar 2004: 24-6). The pollen extracted revealed a decline of Mediterranean vegetation and the dominance instead of olive tree pollen in, broadly, the Roman-Byzantine period. Conversely, the natural vegetation returned in the succeeding Islamic period. Although the original commentators saw this in economic terms as Roman-Byzantine farmers planting more olives on cleared land, Issar and Zohar (2004: 24) have argued that the evidence supports the interpretation that the driving force was not economics but opportunity created by a moister, more suitable environment for olives.

As is well-known, the Dead Sea is a terminal lake (Fig. 3.11). Water from springs or fed by rainfall into streams and rivers within the catchment area, passes through a few significant

Gerasa and the Decapolis

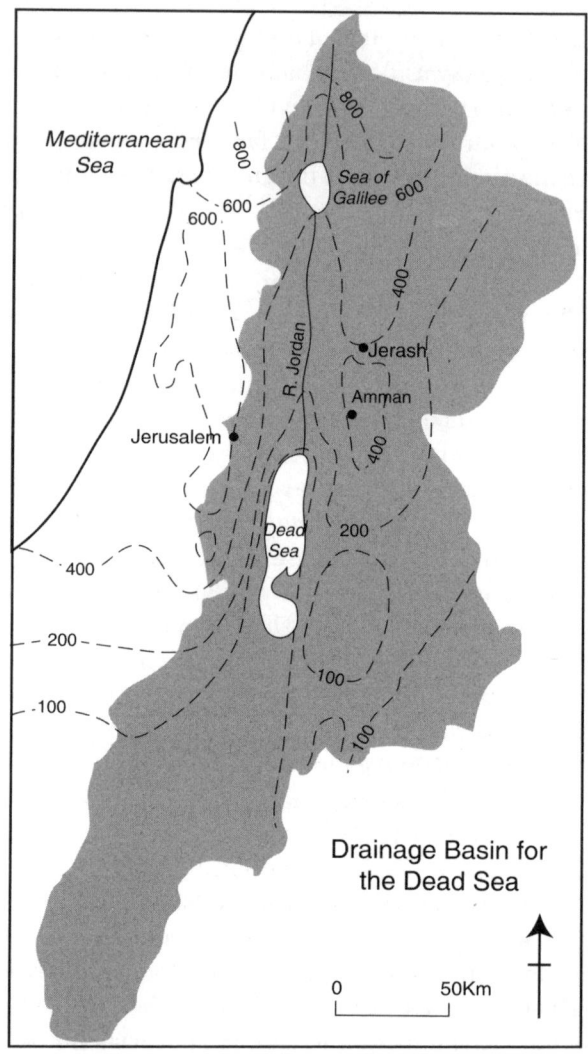

Fig. 3.11. Drainage basin of the Dead Sea (after Bookman et al. 2004: Fig. 1B).

3. The natural and human landscape and environment

rivers (Yarmuk, Zarqa, Jordan, Mujib) and freshwater lakes (Hula, Galilee). Eventually it reaches the Dead Sea from which the only natural outlet is evaporation.

Since the 1960s the level of the Dead Sea has dropped lower than at any time for millennia because of water extraction from its feeders (Issar and Zohar 2004: 28-9). There are two ways of exploiting this. First, sediment layers on the lake bottom reflect the salinity of the water above: more salt in the sediment = less, more saline, water; and vice versa. Second, terraces around its shore preserve a pattern of previous highs and lows and often also contain rich organic material, deposited within relatively short times of entering the sea, which can be carbon-dated to provide absolute dates in an otherwise relative chronology. The exciting feature of recent studies has been the realization that these terraces reflect the rainfall pattern in the catchment basin. A check is possible because of the existence of a rainfall measure for Jerusalem beginning in 1847. Analysis of it alongside more recent records for the Dead Sea has given confidence that the pattern there reflects the situation across the entire headwaters collection area of the Dead Sea (Enzel et al. 2003: 264-6) and that it correlates, too, with northern Jordan (Touchan and Hughes 1999). Overall there is a broad synchronicity between measured rainfall in recent times and the terraces formed along the Dead Sea. Highs and lows in lake level are associated with average rainfall readings of *c.* 650 mm and *c.* 445 mm (Bookman (Ken-Tor) 2004: 570).

For present purposes the most interesting results are those which indicate that there was a low level of at least 407 m below sea level in the Dead Sea in the period *c.* 690-410 BC. Levels then rose during the third and second centuries BC reaching a high in the first century BC of as much as 12.5 m above the earlier low. There was a further high level in the mid-fourth century AD and then from the fifth century AD until at least the ninth century there was a long period of low levels.

In 1989, one commentator concluded that there was no sound basis for believing in a climate change of the significance described above (Rubin 1989). Evidence has accumulated in support of the contrary position and now we have a powerful survey of the archaeological evidence that there *was* a significant increase in rainfall in, broadly, the Roman period (Hirschfeld 2004). Some of Hirschfeld's items are no more than suggestive (as he recognizes) but others are persuasive and collectively they all point in the same direction. The broader significance for this study is this. There is good reason to believe that the climatic fluctuations detectable in Israel apply also to northern Jordan. The range in the fluctuations is impossible to calculate with any great accuracy but seems large enough to make a powerful difference especially in marginal farming areas. Regions of pre-desert barely able to support barley cultivation could become suitable for wheat while previously quite well-watered areas could become even more attractive for olive or grape cultivation if rainfall increases (but cf. Lucke et al. forthcoming). Conversely, a reversion to lower precipitation would soon force a retreat from marginal areas and a re-assessment of growing especially thirsty plants elsewhere. The possible significance of all this for the region will be discussed in ch. 9.

3.7. Discussion

Water is commonly seen as the crucial factor in human use of the region. But there are two other strands of equal and interconnected importance: soils and climate. Water can, if necessary, be taken to arable soils or harvested to concentrate it where cropping is possible. But soils, too, can be harvested to some extent by terracing hillsides and building cross walls on wadis or planting or maintaining vegetation or crops that bind and hold soil. Fossilized versions of the first two can be seen widely in the region. Climate – in this case essentially precipi-

3. The natural and human landscape and environment

tation and sunshine – is vital for the support of crops, pasturage and ripening.

Pollen analysis is becoming increasingly important for the region but is still in its infancy. The potential is revealed by the Sea of Galilee core but it is ambiguous. Moreover, Bottema and van Zeist (1981: 115) interpreted a pollen diagram derived from a core taken from Hula Lake further north to give a similar pattern but with the olive peak ending when the Roman period commences! As this is earlier and is based on unpublished research, the Galilee results may be more reliable. Very recent research, mainly by Israeli scholars, has provided powerful and increasingly persuasive evidence in support of significant changes in precipitation which must be taken into account now by historians and archaeologists. There are, of course, two obvious weaknesses. First, we cannot measure with accuracy what the changes in Dead Sea level would mean in terms of annual precipitation levels or even of broad percentages of increase or decrease. Nor, given the nature of the Dead Sea terraces, can we do more than see broad patterns without knowing detailed fluctuations within long periods of 'high' or 'low'. Second is the problem of dating. Numerous C14 dates were obtained from Dead Sea organic material but the dates themselves are quite broad and, even more worrying, '... the time interval between the beginning of the radiocarbon decay and the deposition of the organic debris is short in the Dead Sea arid environment, from less than a few decades to no more than two centuries; i.e. the radiocarbon age of the organic debris approximately dates the age of the deposition in the section' (Bookman (Ken-Tor) 2004: 565). The combination of the imprecision of C14 dates in the first place and the possibility that vegetation might take up to two centuries to reach its deposition place, is a serious limitation in constructing nuanced history (ch. 9).

4

Settlement

4.1. Hellenistic beginnings, c. 300-50 BC

In c. 300 BC the ancient cities of the Phoenicians and Jews along the Levant coast were recovering from the impact of Alexander's conquest and set for development. Beyond these, the new cities of Hellenistic Syria had taken root with Antioch, Seleucia, Apamea and a score of others, populated by hundreds of thousands of 'Greek' colonists, dominating the landscape of northern Syria (Grainger 1990: 100 estimates as many as half a million). Little can be said of rural settlement.

In contrast, settlement in NWJ was very limited in scale, extent and type. There were urban centres but they were modest affairs – Bronze and Iron Age Tall Jarash, for example, was a mere 8 ha. There is little evidence for rural settlement but every reason to suppose it was modest – ground surveys record small numbers of sites from the Pre-Classical Iron Age.

Two and half centuries later, NWJ had achieved the first stage of its transformation. Several new Hellenistic cities had appeared in the second century BC, some on the sites of Iron Age predecessors as at Pella, Gerasa and Philadelphia. Evidence for their extent and character remains fragmented and uncertain, but they had plainly grown beyond the level of Iron Age *tell* sites to achieve a measure of civic development. Literary sources underscore the existence and significance of most of these urban centres, whose names and hints of character appear most notably in the pages of Josephus' late first-century AD histories. Ironically, however, the physical traces of the places are mod-

4. Settlement

est. Worse still, evidence for rural settlement is largely confined to references in Josephus to named villages. For example, the Dulayl/Zarqa Survey which had found nine rural sites of the Iron Age had none at all of the Hellenistic period.

Period	Sites	Adjusted score (where Iron Age = 100)
Palaeolithic	17	
Neolithic	6	
Chalcolithic (4500-3300 = 2200 years)	2.5	11
Early Bronze Age (3300-1950 = 1350)	9.5	70
MB/ LB (1950-1200 = 750)	2	27
Iron Age (1200-300 = 900)	**9**	**100**
Hellenistic (332-63 = 269)	0	0
Roman (63 BC – AD 324 = 386)	15.5	402
Byzantine (324-640 = 316)	17.5	550
Umayyad (640-750 = 110)	6	550
Abbasid (750-979 = 229)	3	130
Ayyubid/ Mamluk (1174-1516 = 342)	20	580
Ottoman (1516-1918 = 402)	2	50

Table 4.1. Sites recorded by the Dulayl/ Zarqa Survey (from Kennedy 2000).

4.2. Early Rome, c. 50 BC – AD 200

Rome seized control in 63 BC and settlement began to change dramatically. A generation of turmoil followed the Roman takeover, then two or more generations when parts of the region were in the hands of Rome's surrogate Herod the Great and his descendants. All of Herod's family took a keen interest in urbanization and urban development. In NWJ, new urban centres were founded at Livias, Besimoth and Abila in the Peraea, although all were small. On the other hand, the generous gifts of public buildings to cities of Syria seems not to have extended to the cities beyond the Jordan, even Gadara, under Herodian control for many years. Beyond the Peraea lay the Nabataean kingdom. Towns developed at Madaba and Hisban and, far to the northeast in the Hauran, a new city was developed in the first century BC at Bostra. However, the major changes in NWJ took place under Roman rule. It is most easily documented for the cities by means of tables (Table 4.2).

*

A quintessential building of a Greek city long before Alexander's time had been the theatre, and the Greek world abounds in examples. Documentary sources for Hellenistic Syria (and indeed Babylonia and contemporary Egypt) make clear that plays and other theatre entertainment were staged and were popular (Wootton 2000: ch. 3). Yet we have not a single clear example of a theatre from *anywhere* in Hellenistic Syria. That all changed under Roman rule, not least in the Decapolis where every city had at least one theatre or odeon, and Gerasa and Gadara each had a third small theatre nearby. Although dating is usually problematic, the pattern is clear: these theatres are in every case the work of the Roman period and they are overwhelmingly constructed in the late first and second centuries AD with final developments in the early third century.

Theatres are, of course, just one type of structure, yet they are revealing for what their construction implies. The people of Hellenistic Syria had higher civic priorities than constructing places of entertainment, but from the mid-first century AD onwards, civic communities, having provided for necessities in their building programme (defences, paved streets, drainage, record buildings etc.), were turning one after another to recreational building.

Further insights into the development of the cities can be seen by looking at the public buildings of just Gerasa alone. What the list reveals is the period when monumental struc-

4. Settlement

Place	Date	Diameter	Capacity (approx)
Abila	?	73 m	?
Adraha	?	?	?
Canatha	2nd cent. AD	25 m	800
Capitolias? (Beit Ras)	recently found – undated	?	?
Damascus	?	?	?
Dion	?	20 m	
Gadara (North)	?	61 m	?
Gadara (West)	?	40 m	?
Hammat Gader	2nd/ 3rd cent. AD	35 m	1000
Gerasa (South)	late 1st cent. AD	76	4700
Gerasa (North)	2nd half 2nd cent. AD	44 m	1600
Gerasa (Birketein)	late 2nd and 3rd cent. AD	28 m	1000
Pella	late 1st/ early 2nd cent. AD. Dedicated AD 90/91	31 m	1000
Philadelphia (Large)	2nd half 2nd cent. AD	74 m	6000
Philadelphia (Small)	2nd half 2nd cent. AD	36 m	1200
Scythopolis (Large)	late 2nd/ early 3rd cent. AD	82 m	6000
Scythopolis (Small)	?	12+ m	
Bostra	2nd quarter 2nd cent. AD	67 m	6000/9000
Caesarea	Herod the Great	62 m	3500-4000
Sepphoris	Post-70/ early 2nd cent. AD	74 m	4500
Petra	Aretas IV (9 BC – AD 40)	69 m	3000

Table 4.2. Theatres in the Decapolis and adjacent areas (largely after Segal 1995: 98-101).

tures, or monumentalised versions of existing structures, were erected. Once again, the work is overwhelmingly of the later first century AD to the early to mid-third century (Table 2.1). But we should not be misled by these dates. The fall-off in construction in the mid-third century need not imply an economic decline. By then the 'architectural furniture' of these cities was essentially complete.

A final indicator underscores the transformation. At 8 ha, Iron Age Tall Jarash was a few hundred people at most; the area within the defences of Graeco-Roman Gerasa is 80 ha – probably several thousand people (see ch. 5.3-4).

4.3. Opening up the interior: communications and security, AD 200-350

Roads were already in existence long before the Hellenistic period. The road that ran north from the Wadi Mujib past Iron Age Tall Jarash was part of the ancient Biblical King's Highway. Recent work on some ancient tracks east of Jarash suggests they may date as early as the Bronze Age. The Hellenistic period doubtless had its roads and routes but it is the Romans who are most visible in the construction of great highways.

Roman roads are often distinctive: a constructed all-weather surface, kerbs on either side and central spine, culverts and bridges at water courses, road-stations and watch towers and, above all, milestones. These records of construction and repair and often of distances and even placenames, are a vital tool in exploring the chronology of penetration and development in the early Roman period and set it apart from every other period. Dated roads and dated military sites combine to define much of the next stage in the transformation of the region.

Milestones in Jordan are abundant but often bunched geographically and chronologically. Inevitably they are scarcest in the highland area where the duration and intensity of settlement has had the greatest impact on the archaeological record; conversely they are far more numerous in the pre-desert and in the desert can often be followed mile after mile alongside the ancient roads themselves (Fig. 4.1).

4. Settlement

Fig. 4.1. Roman road from Bostra just northwest of Umm e-Quttein. A milestone was found beside the road.

Four phases can be defined (Fig. 4.2 and Table 4.3):

1. First, there are the roads in and around the cities of the highlands. They probably start in the later first century AD but then develop rapidly after the annexation of the Nabataean kingdom (AD 106) and the political reorganization of the region. The two principal highways are the (Scythopolis) – Pella – Gerasa – Philadelphia one and the *Via Nova Traiana*. Collectively the construction and restoration of roads was designed to knit together the urban centres and open up their hinterlands. Perhaps central to the whole network was Gerasa, from which we have several tombstones of the late first century AD attesting a regiment of Thracian cavalry. That in turn strengthens the case for the likely, but so far undetected, road from Gerasa to Bostra direct through Rihab. The latter has military tombstones implying a guard post on a highway but one is for a *beneficiarius*, suggesting a key nodal point.

2. The second phase saw the extension of the official highway

Gerasa and the Decapolis

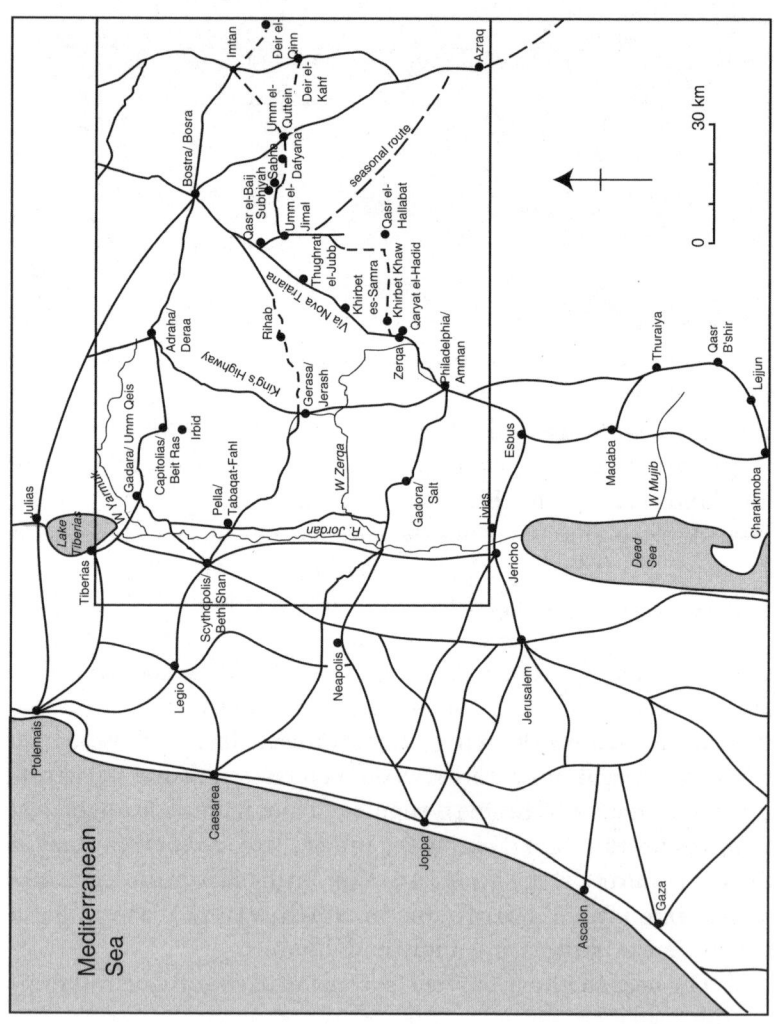

Fig. 4.2. Roman road network in Northwest Jordan (from Kennedy forthcoming).

4. Settlement

	Road	Earliest dates
A	(Caesarea-Scythopolis) – Pella – Gerasa	(69) inferred/proposed 112 – 'restoration'
	Madaba – Philadelphia (KHy/VNT)	111
	Philadelphia – Bostra (VNT)	114
	Gerasa – Philadelphia (KHy)	Flavian? 112 ('restoration')
	Gerasa – Adraha (KHy)	120
	Gerasa – Bostra	?
B	(Ptolemais or Caesarea) – Gadara – Adraha – Bostra – Imtan	162-4?
	Gadora – Pella	181
C	(Jaffna – Jerusalem – Jericho) – Livias – Esbus	212/13
	Imtan – Azraq ('*Via Severiana*')	208/10
	Thuraiya – Ziza – Philadelphia ('*Via Militaris*')	Severus?
D	Jimal – Hallabat	293-305
	Jimal – Quttein – (Kahf)	293-305
	Bostra – Azraq	(293-324)
E	(Ptolemais – Julias) – Bostra	

Table 4.3. Earliest dates on roads in NWJ from milestone evidence (after Kennedy forthcoming).

system to two areas of native communities. In 164 a bridge was built over the Wadi Zedi between Gadara and Bostra and now a milestone of 162 has been reported from what is probably the same road through Salcha to Imtan, 40 kilometres east of Bostra. Imtan is the location of several military texts, some very early (Table 4.5) (Kennedy 2004b: 219-20). Then in the 180s came a road from Gadora to Pella.

3. The third phase is of the very early third century AD.

Unexpectedly late is the road in the Peraea connecting Livias and Esbus (212/3). The surprising development is the road far out into the Basalt Desert, where a '*Via Severiana*' was laid out probably from Imtan through Deir el-Kahf to the Azraq Oasis (208/10). It was evidently part of a major military effort to control a huge water resource, the network of routes through it and the nomads of this inner desert. Inscriptions of almost the same period from forts at the oasis (200; 200/2) and from Qasr el-Hallabat (213/4) are the other arm of the effort. Even more remarkable is the altar of a legionary centurion found at Jauf, 370 km south of Azraq, dated late second/ very early third century AD.

4. The last phase we know of is of the late third/ early fourth century AD. Dates vary, but in essence a surprisingly dense network of roads is attested for the first time, especially in the period of the First Tetrarchs, 293-305. With the exception of the road from Bostra to the Azraq Oasis, all are of only local strategic importance. But once again military inscriptions survive from this period.

Road	Date
(*Via Nova Traiana*	Rebuilding: 285-307)
Umm al-Quttein – Umm al-Jimal	293-305
Umm al-Quttein – Tall Ghariyeh (– Salcha)	317?
Umm al-Jimal – Qasr al-Hallabat	293-305
Milestones found in Umm al-Quttein, some probably for the road from Umm al-Quttein – Bostra	293-305; 305-6; 314-17; 317-24
Road building record at Azraq Oasis	273?

Table 4.4. Dated Tetrarchic milestones in NWJ (largely after Kennedy 1997b).

We can be confident that the purpose of these roads was military. Most of the military inscriptions in Jordan originate in this region and the largest group are of this later period (Table 4.5).

4. Settlement

Place	Date	Key terms
Qasr el-Hallabat	213/4	Castellum novum
Qasr el-Hallabat	529	Kastra (in Greek)
Deir el-Kahf	3rd/4th cent.	
	306	
	348/9	Purgos (in Greek)
	367/75	Castellum
Umm el-Jimal	117/8	Opus valli
Umm el-Jimal	368	Turris
Umm el-Jimal	371	Burgus
Umm el-Jimal	412/3	Kastellos (in Greek)
Umm el-Quttein	2nd/early 3rd cent.	
	348/9 or soon after	
	2nd-4th cent.	
Azraq Duruz	c. 273	Road stone
	c. 300	
	326-33	(Castellum?)
	333	
	323-333	
Qasr el-Uweinid	200/2	Castellum novum
Qasr el-Uweinid	201	Castellum et Praesidium
Umm el-Menara	334	
Qasr el-Ba'ij	411/12	Kastellos (in Greek)
Qal'at Zarqa	253/9	Castra
Imtan, Inat	1st/early 2nd cent.; 1st/2nd cent.; 208; 350; c. 400	

Table 4.5. Military inscriptions from sites in NWJ.

The pattern is clear enough. The picture at first is one of slow development in the first century AD of the highland region where the cities lay. Once the Nabataean kingdom was annexed and the new province created, the pace quickened with a network of roads. Development followed in the Peraea and Southern Hauran in the 160s-180s. Next is the Severan lunge deep into the desert as far as Jauf (Dumata) and including roads and forts at least as far as Azraq. Most of this may well have been abandoned and it is not till the end of the third century that a new and sustained phase begins of roads and military structures. What these structures looked like is clear. This part of Jordan is rich in well-preserved forts and towers and some have been excavated or belong to dated types. In general the forts are relatively small, square or sub-square (Figs 1.2, 2.1, 2.2 and 4.5) (Kennedy 2001c: 188; Fig. 17.10). For example, that at Umm el-Jimal is about 1 ha in size and dated by excavation to c. AD 300. What is important, however, is less the details than the implication. The forts and roads reveal a significant penetration of the pre-desert, of the fertile Southern Hauran and even of the Basalt Desert to some extent. In broad terms this is happening in the period of the First Tetrarchy (286-305) and continuing through the reign of Constantine (324-37).

The impact of this development will have been profound. Doubtless all of these cities were already linked by roads of some kind but new, formalized, all-weather roads with bridges, watch posts, relay stations, and milestones were a significant improvement and one with wider ramifications. Even more than in Italy, perhaps, the new roads would be 'a symbol of the conquest and organization of newly-won territory' striking off in a way that seemed 'to tame the irregularities of the natural landscape' (Zanker 2000: 29). Within a short period the populations of the major cities found themselves firmly anchored to one another by clear, formal roads which came to dominate their worlds but also implied through their very character security and stability. Many rural dwellers, too, will have found a Roman road thrusting past or even through their fields.

Beyond the cities the impact could have been greater still in a landscape with limited vegetation and historically far less developed. The Severan road slicing through the Basalt Desert

4. Settlement

to the Azraq Oasis was a massive intrusion into the world of nomad and trader.

This same period and place witnessed another remarkable development – the appearance of tens of thousands of graffiti evidently scratched by nomads on outcrops and portable rocks. They seem to end about the time the road system is being developed, forts built in greater numbers and the region poised for a significant growth in settlement (ch. 6.6).

4.4. A 'world of villages'... and churches, AD 350-600

Within the increasingly Christian Roman empire, places associated with Christ and his early disciples became magnets for pilgrims. The 'Holy Land', a relative backwater till then, experienced a rapid development with a new religious architecture as churches, monasteries and convents were erected and pious ascetics found homes in the 'wildernesses'.

Urbanization had peaked but the bulk of the population still lived in the countryside and the period is characterized by the emergence of villages as common modes of settlement throughout the Near East. Indeed, despite the fragmented evidence, we have a remarkably lengthy tally of village names. In the case of Apamea in northern Syria the list runs to 48 (Balty and Balty 1983: 57-9). Ancient authors often refer to villages. Josephus presents a view of Palestine as a landscape strewn with villages, and the *Onomasticon* frequently names villages on both sides of the Jordan. Then there is the archaeological evidence. The so-called 'Dead Cities' of the limestone massif of northern Syria are in fact villages, at least 700 of them. Alongside the written evidence there is now an immense corpus of data for actual individual villages in Palestine (Hirschfeld 1997). In the south of Syria there are the scores of villages in the Hauran. Collectively the evidence is considerable and led Millar to characterize the region as 'a world of villages'; there may have been several thousand villages from Mesopotamia to the Negev.

Villages are common in NWJ and, as elsewhere in the Near East, seem to reach a peak in numbers, size and development in this late Roman period. Fortunately there is growing interest in villages in Jordan. As far as the highlands and the urban region are concerned, at this stage it can be little more than impressionistic. A topographic map of Jordan has hundreds of modern villages with the place name element 'khirbat' and, where fieldwork has been conducted among the houses of these villages, the traces are frequently suggestive of settlements more extensive than farmsteads and more often than not belonging to the LCM. In NWJ there has now been significant excavation in recent years at several such villages. It seems that the landscape beyond the urban centres was one largely of villages rather than farmsteads. In the Highlands of Ajlun and the Belqa three stand out. **Yajuz**, 8 km from Amman/ Philadelphia on the Roman road to Gerasa (Fig. 4.3). As so often, the focus has been on the churches but other buildings are now being explored revealing a place of some 20 ha with well-built houses and some agricultural activity inside the village. Then there is the remarkable village at **Umm er-Resas** south of Amman (Fig. 4.4). It is 5 ha and includes not just the civilian settlement but the large military camp which was later occupied by civilians too. The ten churches stand out. Texts trace its settlement from at least AD 41 (Nabataean) through Roman and Byzantine to Christian church mosaics of the eighth century – a marvellous example of continuity of occupation, including deep into the Umayyad period.

The significant development, however, is in the image emerging of the village landscape of the pre-desert. In this case it is not just the familiar and highly important village world of the Hauran charted so evocatively by the Princeton Expeditions to Syria (PES) a century ago but the accumulating evidence of

4. Settlement

Fig. 4.3. Aerial view of Yajuz (APA02/ 31.34; 2 October 2002).

Fig. 4.4. Aerial view of Umm er-Resas (APA98/ 34.26; 20 May 1998).

villages throughout the pre-desert often underlying the modern ones. In this instance, however, because the modern villages are much more recent than those in the highlands further west, the traces of their ancient predecessor are more evident. About 3 km east of the modern Jordanian city of Zarqa lies the site of **Khirbet Khaw** (Fig. 2.1). The air photograph shows a marvellous range of structures: a small fort of 1 ha, a caravanserai on its west and the outlines of houses on the slope below these. A total village size of 5.5 ha/ 13.5 acres. The fort is probably *c.* AD 300.

This account of individual villages could be added to easily, albeit with less detail. A striking feature of so many of them is the frequency with which churches are encountered. A church in every village is to be expected but in several instances the numbers are puzzling. Fifteen churches within the 80 ha of Gerasa may not surprise unduly, but the same number is found in the 30 ha of Umm el-Jimal and in the sprawling village of Rihab. There are at least ten at Umm er-Resas, a site of 5 ha. Of course the multiple churches need not be in contemporary use but the numbers represent a phenomenon that requires more attention. Many of them have mosaic floors, often incorporating a text with a date.

Finally, we may roughly gauge the intensity of village settlement in the pre-desert by mapping the traces of ancient cisterns. Simple farmsteads might require more than one cistern, but Fig. 3.11 shows regular concentrations of multiple cisterns in and around the modern villages. Plainly these are the locations of ancient settlements with multiple houses – villages.

What lay beyond the villages in the highlands and pre-desert? In the highland area there are hints of farmsteads of the period. Often they are implied rather than visible – ancient rock-cut cisterns and a scatter of pottery are suggestive of structures now re-used. Especially suggestive – and increasingly common – are rock-cut presses for oil and grapes.

Further east, air photography has revealed a number of

4. Settlement

Fig. 4.5. A rectilinear 'farm' in the Basalt Desert south of Umm el-Jimal. It is overlying seemingly old structures similar to those showing more faintly in the background (APA98/SL9.34, 12 May 1998).

rectilinear structures which are probably farms, usually lying beside seasonal water courses, wadis (Fig. 4.5). No less interesting is the faint trace in the background of this photograph of curvilinear structures which may represent predecessors to the bolder rectilinear one. Rainfall was slighter in this part of the pre-desert and the emphasis had to be given to harvesting water to irrigate small fields (ch. 3.4). The procedure is well-known from the Negev Desert and from Algeria but is also found in NWJ. Low walls were built across the alignment of wadis – 'cross-wadi walls' – which created 'fields' and obtained water sufficient to cultivate cereals (Fig. 3.8). In this instance, pottery on the curvilinear structures beside the fields is broadly late Roman to early Umayyad. Around the small Nabataean-Roman-Umayyad town of Umm el-Jimal, air photo interpretation has revealed traces of a hundred, possibly as many as 200 'farms' of this kind. It is likely that detailed interpretation of the photographs for a wider area will populate the landscape with many more such structures (Kennedy 1997a; 2001b).

It is common now to view settlement in this period as one that saw a shift from city to countryside. The absence of much monumental building in the cities is a key indicator of that. But it may be misleading. The number and richness of churches in the cities, many with elaborate mosaic floors, reveals a vibrant building programme (Table 4.6). There is no compelling reason to view the towns as in decline in prosperity and population size except, perhaps, in relative terms as the countryside prospered.

A feature of fundamental importance on which there is now an emerging consensus is the shift in the mode of transport. The form of roads, depictions of vehicles in art and literary references all confirm that wheeled transport was common in the early Roman period. Bullocks drawing two-wheeled wagons with solid wheels and donkeys or asses pulling four-wheeled spoked wagons, are the common combinations. The halt in evidence for road construction noted in the previous section is paralleled by the growth in references to pack animals and disappearance of wheeled transport throughout the Near East.

4.5. Ruling from the margins, AD 600-850

The Islamic conquest of the Near East brought major shifts which influenced settlement patterns. The Christian holy places were now supplemented by a new religious geography. That led some of the faithful to Jerusalem but it caused many more to follow a regular route *through* northern Jordan to holy places in distant Arabia. On the other hand, the political centre of gravity was now nearby in Damascus and the Umayyad dynasty's power base lay with the tribes of Arabia including the nomads. Finally, the trade which had once spanned a frontier was now largely contained *within* the new empire. For the

4. Settlement

Structure	Date
Cathedral	2nd half of 4th cent.? (AD 365?)
(Shrine of St Mary	2nd quarter of 5th cent. or later)
Apostles, Prophets and Martyrs	AD 464/5
St Theodore	AD 494-6
Procopius Church	AD 526-7
Complex:	
St George	AD 529-30
St John the Baptist	AD 531
SS Cosmas and Damian	AD 533
Synagogue Church	AD 530-1
SS Peter and Paul	AD 540
(Southwest Chapel	2nd quarter of 6th cent.)
Bishop Isaiah Church	AD 558
Mortuary Church	AD 565
Propylaea and Diakonia	AD 565
Church of Bishop Marianos	AD 570
Church on the Intermediate Terrace	6th cent.
St Genesius	AD 611
Churches on the Terrace of Temple of Zeus	Undated
Octagonal Church	Undated
Elias	Undated
Maria and Soreg	Undated

Table 4.6. The principal public buildings of Gerasa: second phase.

people of NWJ all these factors surely brought about a marked re-orientation of their world-view.

There was an old notion of rapid collapse of urban civilization and the overall shrinkage of settlement as supposedly destructive desert-dwellers seized control. In recent years, however, several sites in the region have been shown conclusively to have a significant Umayyad phase of occupation including new construction. It is clear, too, in the cities, not least Gerasa where excavation has revealed one of the few town houses of any period and a major mosque in the very heart (Walmsley and Damgaard 2005). Finally, of course, it is clear in the more mundane record of potsherds from the scores of sites of all kinds recorded by ground surveys (Table 4.1). The most striking feature of the Umayyad period, however, is the development of new sites – or, rather, of new types of settlement on existing sites, sometimes on a much grander scale.

Qasr el-Hallabat (Fig. 1.2) is almost exactly at the point where pre-desert, Basalt Desert and Chert Desert meet (cf. ch. 1.1). Earlier phases included settlement in the Nabataean period and a Roman fort. The final, Umayyad, phase saw the site transformed into a 'Desert Castle', a residence for an Umayyad prince or grandee. There are major examples of such structures in Syria, but there is a particular concentration in NWJ. Indeed, it has been observed that the continuation of widespread settlement into the Umayyad period is especially notable in the Belqa and Hauran (H. Kennedy 1992) (cf. ch. 2.3).

Umayyad Hallabat was ornate: acroteria and crows-step blocks on the upper reaches, relief carvings of tendrils and rosettes and even a bird. Several of the rooms around the internal courtyard were provided with mosaic floors employing gold leaf, while the walls were frescoed. A few metres away stood an early mosque. Scattered all around were multi-roomed, rectilinear houses, especially around the huge reservoir. And a little further away still lay an embanked garden, divided into plots with walls and sluice gates between. About 3 km to the east was a small bath building.

What is significant about these sites is that while a few have a Roman predecessor, sometimes military, more commonly modest settlement, many are on new locations; they are on the fringe of the pre-desert or in the desert including the Chert Desert (Kha-

4. Settlement

raneh, Amra and Mushash). Most did not survive the collapse of the dynasty. As H. Kennedy (1992) observed: 'the Umayyad *qusur* were the product of peculiar and particular social and economic conditions which were not replicated at other times.'

Place	Date	Features
(Philadelphia-Amman		Gubernatorial Palace)
Qasr Mshatta	743	'Winter Palace' of Caliph Walid II; 144 x 144 m
Qasr et-Tuba	743-4	Desert palace, 145 x 70 m. Incomplete
Qasr Mushash	(4th-7th cent.) Umay	18 structures over 4 sq km area: qasr (26 x 26 m), bath suite, buried buildings, reservoir, cisterns, gardens?
Qasr el-Kharaneh	c. 710	Fortress (?)/ audience residence, c. 25 x 25 m, two storeys
Qasr Amra	c. 705-15	Audience chamber and elaborately decorated bath suite
Azraq Shishan	Umayyad	Irrigated garden (and mansion?), huge reinforced reservoir and encircling wall for oasis pools
Qasr Ain es-Sil	Umayyad	Mansion, c. 17 m sq, two storeys with bath suite, oil press and ovens; farm; hydraulic works; wall 2.5 km+
Qasr el-Hallabat	(Nab, Roman) Umayyad	Mansion, 38 m sq, two storeys, mosaics, frescoes, mosque, houses, reservoir, cisterns, irrigated garden; bath suite 3 km away
Umm el-Walid	(Nab, Rom) Umayyad	Roman village developed in Umayyad period: East Qasr = 71 x 71 m; two other *qusur*; two large dams and farm with wine press nearby
El-Fedein	(Late Roman) Umayyad	Large house; bath suite (?); mansion
Qastal	Umayyad	Qasr, 68 x 70; early mosque; bath suite (?) with mosaics; reservoirs, cisterns; large dam
Khan es-Zebib	Umayyad?	Qasr 44 x 49 m; caravanserai
('Qubbash')	Umayyad	Named in ancient sources as a royal estate in the Balqa

Table 4.7. Principal Umayyad 'rural' sites in NWJ. Evocative aerial views of many can be seen in Kennedy and Bewley 2004, esp. ch. 12.

4.6. Discussion

Viewed as a series of 'snapshots', two or three centuries apart, one can trace a significant change overtake the settlement pattern of this region. At the outset it is poorly developed and permanent settlements are few, mainly small and restricted in large part to the highlands and Belqa. A thousand years later it is dramatically different. Why did that happen? And why did it take the forms that it did? There is no reason to believe in a single overarching explanation. Politically the region underwent major changes and the arrival of first Christianity then Islam as major world religions displacing paganism were important. But there had been significant developments before Christianity and there is in any case good reason to avoid mono-causal explanations. One element may be explored here – albeit speculatively.

In the Umayyad period, a persuasive case has been made that it was because NWJ was precisely the region in which the dynasty had extensive lands and, against the background of a weak royal fiscal system, was compelled to exploit its lands to the full to maximize revenue. That the dynasty has extensive estates in these regions is undeniable; *why* that should be so seems not to have received any attention. One possibility we may investigate to enable us to explore still further the question of why settlement became so extensive in the late Roman-Umayyad period is that it is an outcome of the forms of land tenure in place in the Roman period. In a nutshell, the Umayyad family may have held extensive estates in this region precisely because there had been a concentration of imperial estates there when they seized the region. The possibility must remain largely conjecture but there are some hints at it. First there is the entry in George of Cyprus giving a placename Saltus [= imperial estate] and the possibility that its form is preserved still in the modern Jordanian city of Salt (ancient

4. Settlement

Gadora). George also records a Saltus Bataneos in, probably, the region north of the Hauran (Jones 1971: 288-9). Second there is the concentration of boundary markers in the Hauran from the Tetrarchic period. The implications of these are not well-understood but one possibility is that they are the outcome of defining or redefining imperial property (cf. Graf 2001: 227). A final hint may be seen in the landscape itself. Aerial views of the Hauran show a pattern to fields in some places that is quite different from the irregular form of organic development and growth found elsewhere in the same area (Fig. 4.6). Long strip fields of a regular form can be traced in some parts of the Southern Hauran and in another area there are rectangular fields which again suggest a policy of land division being applied to a large area to suit colonists (cf. Kennedy 1985). Dating such field systems is as yet impossible. The best hints, however, lie in the settlements which are overwhelmingly of the LCM. There is also the possibility of settlement of Gothic colonists in the third-fourth centuries (Kennedy 2004b: 219-20). Finally, of course, the Southern Hauran is precisely the area in which so much of a broad landscape is divided between villages, large and small, and without evidence of a city to which they may be attributed. Except, of course, Bostra, the seat of governor, legion and administration.

A final speculation might be to ask: Did the Romans in AD 106 take over a city at Bostra whose surrounding lands were largely Nabataean royal property which passed to the emperor as imperial estates? Or was potentially arable land in the 'possession' of nomads who could be dispossessed or settled as colonists of some kind? And did the imperial authorities then lay claim to lands more widely whose future development could be seen? That is precisely what we hear happening 1800 years later when the extension of security and construction of the Hedjaz Railway in northern Transjordan led the Ottoman authorities to claim wide areas:

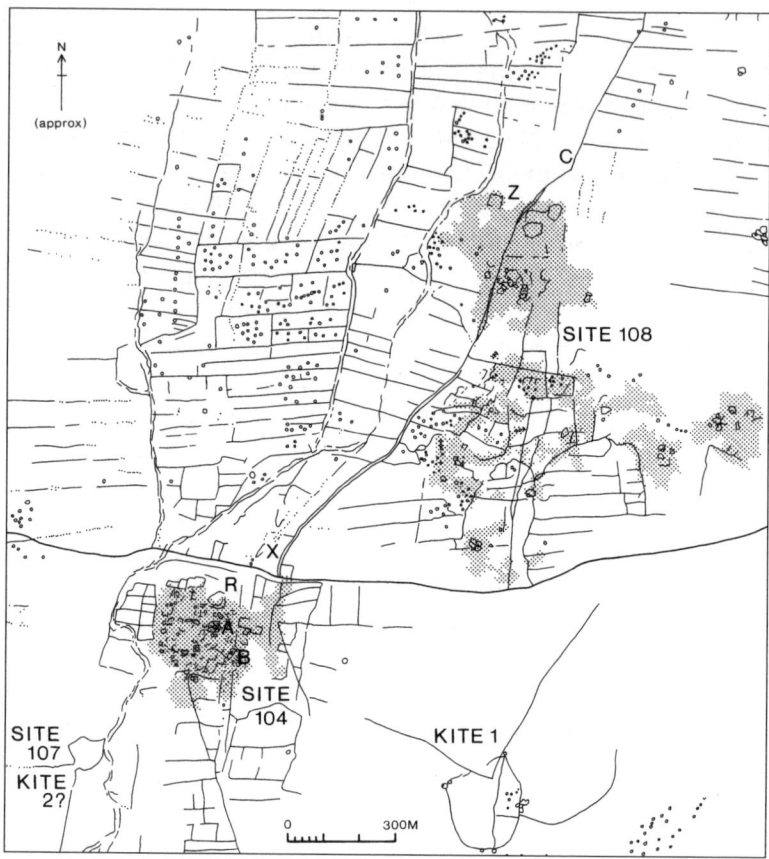

Fig. 4.6. Settlement patterns in the Southern Hauran (from Kennedy and Freeman 1995: 53, Fig. 17). Air photo interpretation and ground survey suggested a Middle Bronze Age site beginning in the north then re-appearing in the central area (Site 108) as a Roman village with largely early Roman (first century BC to third century AD) sherds. Site 104 is another Roman village with largely early dates. Both have some later pottery and there are a few Umayyad sherds. The settlements are at the heart of a system of fossilised field walls within which is embedded at least one prehistoric 'kite' (animal trap). Water was harvested by at least one channel into cisterns and a large open reservoir at Site 104. Ceramics included imports – some Nabataean, African Red Slip (third-fourth centuries AD) and an amphora (fifth-eighth centuries AD). This pattern is repeated throughout much of this marginal pre-desert region.

4. Settlement

... During the five years since I had visited this district [the communities of Salt and Madaba] had pushed forward the limit of cultivation two hours' ride to the east and proved the value of the land so conclusively that when the Hajj railway was opened through it the Sultan laid hands on a great tract stretching as far south as Ma'an, intending to convert it into a chiflik, a royal farm (Bell 1907: 22-6).

5

Population and people

> ... population size matters, and is of more than antiquarian interest. In fact, it can be critical for our perception of the history of some of the most important communities of the classical world. Scheidel 2001b: 50

A. POPULATION SIZE

5.1. Introduction

'How many?' is a simple question yet one whose answer is highly elusive for both Greek and Roman history. We cannot even put numbers to some of the most important places. The population size for the city of Rome at its peak? About one million is the commonly quoted number (e.g. Hopkins 1978: 96-8) but influential voices argue for much less (*c.* 600,000) (Storey 1997) and significantly more (*c.* 1.2 million) (Lo Cascio 1994, 2000, 2001). Even the expression 'at its peak' refers to a period of two or three centuries during which population probably fluctuated widely. The same problem exists for the population of the Roman empire as a whole. There is a consensus that it probably rose across this same 'peak' period from *c.* 45 to *c.* 50-60 million (Hopkins 1999: 646; Frier 2000: 811-13) but one commentator, normally sceptical of higher estimates, concedes that 80 million is possible (Scheidel 2001b: 63n.257). The same scholar notes that historians of more recent, better-documented periods, are incredulous at the wide range and softness of the figures with which ancient historians attempt to work (Scheidel

5. Population and people

2001b: 56-7). The situation gets still worse. Ancient historians have little idea about the structure of ancient populations: urban: rural divide, free: slave, age structure, mortality rates, ethnic groups and, of course, even less in most cases about changes in such patterns. When one reads assertions that the urban:rural divide was about 15:85 on average across the empire and perhaps as much as 20:80 in the East we must remember that this is no more than an intelligent guess (Hopkins 1999: 647).

5.2. Population numbers

It is a simple matter to get a broad impression of relative human numbers for NWJ despite problems of dating and the visibility of artefacts (ch. 4). There are half a dozen relatively small 'cities' of the Hellenistic/ Nabataean period and a thin and geographically limited rural population. For the Roman period we can identify a dozen cities, many much larger now, numerous villages and farms and a much more widespread rural pattern extending into the pre-desert and Southern Hauran. These same two regions also bear the traces of datable Roman forts and roads which even extend into the Basalt Desert beyond. In short, there is an unmistakable impression of a steep increase in the size, number and extent of settlements. It is clear, too, that much of this high level of settlement continued well into the succeeding Umayyad period. After that there is a steady decline in numbers of sites. There was a retreat from desert and steppe but also a decline even within the fertile hills and plain regions. Finally, it is widely agreed that the high tide of settlement in scale and extent during the LCM was unparalleled until the very different conditions of the mid-twentieth century (cf. ch. 2.3).

This broad pattern is worth knowing and, even if we cannot define it in terms of actual numbers of people nor even coarse estimates, it immediately suggests important questions we should ask: Why did population rise so steeply and why did it decline? Why was it able to spread so far? Why did it never again come close to such high levels even under the Ottoman empire?

Of course, such an impressionistic approach is pathetically inadequate. Consequently immense efforts have been expended not just on the Near East but throughout the Roman empire to try to calculate reasonably precise absolute numbers for individual cities, regions and entire provinces. As Table 5.1 shows, there have been a number of such estimates for a few of the cities of the Jordanian Decapolis.

We need now to look briefly at the methods available for estimating the populations of places, regions and provinces and the reliability of the results. We do in fact have a few seemingly precise numbers in literary sources for populations in the East. Many, however, are of the kind reported by Caesar for populations in Gaul in the 50s BC or by the first century AD Jewish historian, Flavius Josephus for participants in Jewish religious festivals. Most have now been shown to be fantastic or hopelessly unreliable and need not be discussed (Henige 1998a: 214-42; 1998b; McGing 2002; cf. Kennedy 2006b). A few numbers seem more reliable. For Alexandria, Diodorus Siculus (late first century BC), says that he obtained a figure of 300,000 from 'the men who keep the registers of the inhabitants' (17.52.6). Population size for Egypt – excluding Alexandria – is given by Josephus as 7.5 million (*Bellum Judaicum* 2.385). Josephus' report is now generally distrusted; Diodorus is also probably unreliable (Rathbone 1990: 103-7). Next there is the handful of cities around the empire for which we are given precise population numbers or numbers from which we may infer the population. Once again, most are, at best, problematic (Kennedy 2006b). One, however, close to NWJ, seems different.

An inscription gives the career steps of Q. Aemilius Secundus

5. Population and people

City	Area	Population	Source
Abila		12,000	Lucke forthc.
Abila (Peraea)			
(Arbela?)			
Adraha			
Besimoth			
Bostra		5,000	Sartre 2001: 701-2
Capitolias			
(Dion?)			
Esbus			
Gadara			
Gadora			
Gerasa	85 ha	20-25,000 plus territory	Khouri 1986: 29
Livias			
Madaba			
Pella			
Philadelphia			
Scythopolis	150+ ha 110 ha	44,000-50,000	Foerster, Tsafrir ARAM: 117f McGing 2002: 106 n. 64
Umm el-Jimal	30 ha	7,000-10,000 2,500; '3,000 might be closer to the mark' 6000-8000 (in 6th cent.)	Butler 1913: 195 De Vries 1998: 109-11 Butcher 2003: 106

Table 5.1. City population estimates.

which include the report that he was sent by (P. Sulpicius) Quirinius, governor of Syria *c*. AD 6, to conduct a census of the state of Apamea in Syria and that he counted 117,000 *hom(ines) civ(ium)*. As so often with such texts, the meaning is disputed. Traditionally it has been interpreted to refer to adult males only which then implies a total population for the state – town and territory – of *c*. 500,000. A few dissenting voices have been heard and a case has now be made that this census number in fact implies a much smaller population, perhaps 125-130,000 (Kennedy 2006b). Such an outcome is important. Of the four great cities of Hellenistic Syria – the Tetrapolis – Antioch was by far the largest but Apamea had been the military headquarters of the Seleucid kingdom and had a city wall enclosing 250 ha. It may have also been the base – or close to the base of one of the Syrian legions in the early first century AD (Tacitus *Annals* II.79.3). In the absence of much else, one may extrapolate in very crude terms from the conclusion about population size for this single city to the population of the province. At half a million a large provincial population was likely – at least five or six million; at an eighth of a million a much smaller population is likely – perhaps as low as two to three million (cf. Kennedy 1996a: 707-8), similar perhaps to the same area in the nineteenth century under Ottoman rule (Jabbur 1995: App. II). Of course, this is the very early Roman imperial period and there is a broad acceptance that population in Syria grew steadily and significantly over the succeeding centuries both because the territory grew in size as a succession of principalities was absorbed but also because settlement became thicker and more widespread.

How can this help for the Decapolis cities and for population sizes in the region as a whole? The short answer is that it can be no more than suggestive. We do not know the territory size of Apamea despite a single boundary marker which implies it stretched far into the steppe. In the Decapolis, Gerasa is now known to have had what appear to be boundary markers on the northeast round to southeast (Seigne 1997). But the overall territory is unknown. As for the other cities, we have still less – Philadelphia shared a boundary with Gerasa; milestone numbering between cities seems to change when the boundary is crossed; and church mosaic inscriptions in the village of Rihab east of Gerasa seem to show it belonging to the diocese of Bostra which gives that city a substantial territory.

All we have to go on for these cities is that in the case of Gerasa we have the complete town wall enclosing an area of 85 ha. Using Apamea as a crude guide, that might imply a popu-

5. Population and people

lation for city and territory at Gerasa of perhaps 40-50,000 people. Of course, this takes no account of important factors such as differences in territory size, extent of arable land, pace of development (Apamea was about 150 years older than Gerasa), the date of the walls (Hellenistic for Apamea and Roman at Gerasa). Nevertheless, it is the best we have to go on at the moment and can be used to obtain some sort of guidelines for population size, distribution and development.

5.3. Northwest Jordan

We have a few pieces of hard evidence to work with. First, we know, with a reasonable degree of confidence the size of the garrison of the province of Arabia in the second century AD. A legion of $c.$ 5000 soldiers was headquartered at Bostra (though detachments of it are attested widely throughout the province and the fortress is surprisingly small: Kermorvant et al. 2003). It has long been accepted that there were also about 5000 auxiliaries, and the newly discovered diploma for Arabia broadly bears that out (Weiss and Speidel 2005) – so, a garrison of about 10,000. Next we have the number of cities in NWJ – 12, although that includes places that were still very small in the second century AD and several that actually belong to Palestine. Third, we have the precise area of one those cities (Gerasa) as defined by its wall circuit. Finally, fieldwork has identified a large number of small towns and villages in the steppe east of the Decapolis cities and in the Southern Hauran beyond. At one of these (Umm el-Jimal) a specific count of houses was possible and led to a suggested population size.

Soldier:civilian ratio

First, there is the question of the likely ratio of soldiers to civilians. There is, of course, a significant difference between

Gerasa and the Decapolis

those provinces with an external frontier and a possibly hostile power beyond and those which are internal, sharing borders only with other provinces. Internal provinces had only enough troops to provide for the needs of the governor and imperial officials; at most, normally only one or two regiments of auxiliary soldiers, a few hundred, perhaps a thousand at most. The ratio of soldier to civilian in so-called military provinces was very different.

We can start with the ratio for the empire as a whole. The army size (including Rome garrison and fleets) was about 400,000 by c. 200 AD. As we have seen (ch. 5.1), estimates for the population size of the empire as a whole favour 50-60 million in the same period, giving a ratio of 1:125 to 1:150; 80 million would give a ratio of 1:200.

Next we can turn to various provinces. During the first two centuries AD we can usually identify the number of legions and auxiliary regiments in almost every province and, assuming each was at its full 'book' strength, calculate the number of soldiers fairly reliably. Much more difficult is the size of population in the same province. This is of course the very difficulty this present discussion is endeavouring to resolve for one region. There have been calculations done for many provinces and, though they are all problematic in various ways, they may be worth pursuing a little further to see what, if any, pattern is visible.

We may begin with Britain. In the second century AD the army was about 60,000 strong (Frere 1987: 301). Estimates of population size have been rising steadily for over 75 years. Collingwood estimated half a million in 1929; the following year Wheeler suggested 1.5 million. In 1967 Frere put forward two million but 20 years later, in the light of the thousands of sites being found from ground and aerial survey, he raised his estimate to three million. Others have thought even that too low and figures as high as six million have been proposed (Millett 1990: 182). For present purposes I shall take four million as the

5. Population and people

figure for the second century. That would imply a ratio of c. 1:65. Of course, Britain, an especially turbulent province, had a particularly large army – perhaps the largest in the empire in the second century. Soldier to civilian ratio may well have been higher than in other military provinces.

In Egypt the garrison of the second century was again about 10,000 in a population now estimated at between four and five million (Scheidel 2001a: 142). A ratio of 1:400 or 1:500. Of course, unlike Britain, Egypt had no significant frontier problems in the second century: great deserts flanked it on east and west and much of the garrison was intended to police the population rather than shield it.

Judaea in the second century was anomalous. It was an internal province with no external threatening power. However, the province was notable for its bloody insurrections and rebelliousness. Hence it had two legions in garrison plus several thousand auxiliaries – perhaps 20,000 in total (cf. Safrai 1994: 456). Population size has been estimated by several scholars but no consensus has emerged. Broshi (1980) argued for about one million but a more recent commentator thought that too low (Safrai 1994: 436-7). At one million, the ratio would be 1:50.

Finally we come to Syria. In the second century there were three legions (c. 15,000) and probably 15,000 auxiliaries (Kennedy and Riley 1990: 44, Table II). If the population was three million by that time, the ratio would be 1:100; if it was as high as five million, the ratio would be 1: 65. For the third century and for all of the provinces of the Near East, Millar speculates that the c. 100,000 soldiers there may have represented a ratio of 1:100 (1993: 527) – i.e. a population of about ten million. Here, of course, Rome confronted the only other great power on its frontiers and troop levels surely allowed for that.

The ratios fluctuate so widely and the special factors in each case are so important that it is not clear what wider lesson may be drawn and how it could be applied to Arabia. At best, we may suppose that Arabia as a whole had a ratio of 1:200 or less; probably much less. At 1:200 the population would be two million. That is surely far too high when modern Jordan has a population of less than 5.8 million (estimate of July 2005).

Population density of cities

We turn next to consider the population density of Gerasa within walls encompassing 85 ha. Walls are, at best, a crude guide to urban size. In the East in some cases they seem to include areas that were perpetual open space (e.g. the ravine of the Wadi Jarash at Gerasa) and tactical advantage might lead builders to include areas that would never be developed and unrealistic ambitions might cause city councils to define their city as they hoped it might be rather than as it ever was.

There is no consensus about what population density figure to apply. Scholars have often turned to some of the densely populated cities of modern times for figures. Rome and its port city of Ostia certainly both had high density housing with people living in tall buildings of two, three or four storeys. Some of the city populations recorded in ancient literature implied very high densities but many of those figures must be treated with caution if not dismissed. Although Rome and Ostia certainly would have been densely settled, there is no good reason to believe that was true of other cities. Some did include two-storey houses and they are preserved to that height in some villages in both Syria and Arabia, but the lower floor was often for animals (below).

There is growing agreement that applying known high spot densities in early modern and modern cities to ancient ones is very misleading. The reality is that density certainly fluctuated over time and densities varied between cities. In such circumstances, the surer methodology is not to pretend we can obtain a reliable figure but to adopt the suggestion of Wilkinson (2003: 42) and apply one or two low densities as guides.

5. Population and people

A second consideration is the likely split between urban (town) and rural (territory) population. Again, we do not know the answer for anywhere in the Roman empire. For Apamea, with a suggested overall population for town and territory of c. 125,000, and an area of 250 ha, an urban density of 100 people per ha would imply c. 25,000 people and c. 100,000 in its territory. That is exactly Hopkins' opinion (1999: 647) that average overall urban: rural split but in the East the proportion was likely to be higher at about 20:80. For early imperial Apamea, a city of 25,000 would be a major centre. If the density was already higher at, say, 200 per ha, we would have a town of c. 50,000 people and a rural population of c. 75,000 with c. 40% of the population in the town. That is double Hopkins' suggested proportion and seems highly implausible when one considers the numbers who would have to be supported from the rural surplus. In the circumstances, a density overall at Apamea in the early first century AD of about 100 people per ha would seem more plausible although that is based on little more than a current preference among many ancient demographers for a minimalist approach to population numbers and the views of one experienced and persuasive commentator. In the early first century AD Apamea was part of a world in which the movement of large surpluses of foodstuffs was only getting underway and may have been still largely dependent on its own hinterland resources.

Other cities in the region are harder to estimate for population. Unlike Gerasa, for none of them do we have a complete wall circuit; in some cases we have fragments of walls which are at best suggestive of overall size. City sizes varied considerably with Livias and Esbus, for example, plainly quite small. For present purposes it is average figures that are of concern.

We do not know which of the figures in Table 5.2 is closest to reality at any point in time. But the numbers can be evaluated for probability. Let us suppose, for example that the lowest

Gerasa and the Decapolis

Cities		Territory/ City + Territory	
Average	Total	10%	20%
5,000	60,000	540,000/ 600,000	240,000/ 300,000
7,500	90,000	810,000/ 900,000	360,000/ 450,000
10,000	120,000	1,080,000/1,200,000	480,000/ 600,000
12,500	150,000	1,350,000/1,500,000	600,000/ 750,000
15,000	180,000	1,620,000/ 1,800,000	720,000/ 900,000

Table 5.2. Projected populations for the twelve cities and their territories in NWJ (Abila, Adraha, Bostra, Capitolias, Esbus, Gerasa, Gadara, Gadora, Livias, Madaba, Pella, Philadelphia).

figures are the nearest to reality. That would imply that this region of NWJ had an overall population of 300,000 people of whom 20% lived in 12 cities whose average population size was 5,000. If true, that might suggest the population of Arabia as a whole (it has a few more cities [Rabba, Characmoab, Petra, Aila] but some of the Decapolis cities being counted here belonged to Palestine) was about 400,000. To police that population and secure it against nomads, the imperial authorities provided a garrison in the second century AD of about 10,000, the great majority of whom – not least the legionaries who made up about half these troops – were based in the north of the region as one might expect. A ratio of one soldier for every 40 people is surely far too high?

But what of the other extreme? An overall population in the region of almost 1.8 million of whom 10% (180,000) lived in cities whose average population was 15,000. Arabia as a whole might then have had a population of *c.* 2.4 million and with a garrison of still 10,000 a ratio of soldier to civilian of 1:240. Moreover, to allow for several very small cities with small populations, we would have to envisage places like Gerasa having much larger ones – perhaps 20-25,000 and a population density of *c.* 250-300 per ha. This number is surely far too high.

Is there any further way that will allow us to evaluate these options? Ideally, one would count actual houses in towns or

5. Population and people

villages and multiply by the likely average size of occupant groups. Precisely this approach was adopted for Pompeii where the crucial evidence for houses actually survives and we can determine how many stories there were and calculate the area within the walls. The two most recent and convincing counts for Pompeii have converged at *c*. 11,000 and *c*. 12,000 respectively, implying a gross density within the walls of only 170-185 per ha, but other calculations have put it in the range 8-12,000 which would bring the figure down at the lower end to *c*. 125 per ha (Scheidel 2001b: 59n.236). In the Near East, we have little evidence for housing in any city and almost nothing at all for those of NWJ. We do, however, have the important evidence for Umm el-Jimal. There one encounters well-preserved two-storey houses which can be explored to reveal stables on the ground floor and living accommodation above. De Vries (1998: 109-11) has counted 128 houses and, allowing 20 people on average to each, concluded the overall population in the sixth to seventh centuries was *c*. 2500-3000. The town is unplanned and rather different from the cities of the region. The area is *c*. 30 ha which would imply on De Vries' calculation a density of *c*. 1:100 or less.

Further north in Syria, the villages of the limestone massif have also been the object of some population calculations. There are some 700 villages throughout the region and 4+ people in each of an average of 100 rooms per village (Foss 1995: 222). The result is *c*. 300,000 people in villages averaging as much as 400-500 people in each. One may doubt that rooms in every house had as many as 4+ people in each, but such calculations are suggestive of a marginal landscape which could support significant stone-built villages and a population which should be measured in the tens of thousands.

A final method attempted for Egypt and Judaea is to define the land available for food production then estimate its carrying capacity (Rathbone 1990). For Egypt it was relatively easy to define the narrow Nile Valley and the major oases. It was more problematic for Judaea where the arable land is less easily identified. It is not as yet possible to define farmable land in NWJ. Even if it were possible, there are great difficulties in determining what ancient yields might have been and it takes no account of the extent to which food might have been imported or exported (cf. Safrai 1994: ch. 6).

5.4. Discussion

It is immediately apparent that we have no reliable guide to the size of population in the region at any point in its history. The only semi-hard number available is that for the army in the second century. The few examples cited above, however, reveal the wide differences there seem to be in soldier:civilian ratios which make it impossible to apply any one of them to Arabia.

With population density we are on slightly firmer ground. Few scholars now would utilize high spot density numbers; indeed, most seem to prefer lower densities of 100 or 200 at most. As we saw, a density in the range 100-200 fits well with detailed calculations for Pompeii with its frequent double storeys and relatively dense buildings. Closer to home, the census figure for Apamea in the very early first century AD makes most sense if the town had a density of closer to 100 than 200. And at Umm el-Jimal the calculation on the basis of house size also points to a density near to 100.

This may be the best one can do for the moment. The tendency for the consensus to move to minimalist figures in recent years together with the insights of Wilkinson regarding the population sizes of Bronze Age towns in Mesopotamia, points to the major towns of NWJ (Gadara, Pella, Capitolias, Abila, Gerasa, Adraha, Bostra, Philadelphia) having populations of 10,000 or less in the second century AD. In contrast, the small towns (Livias, Gadora, Esbus, Madaba) probably had no more than 5000 each. In short, a total urban population of 100,000.

5. Population and people

It is possible all these city numbers increased during the following 500-600 years although it is not necessary to see the increase as a dramatic one. The peak of construction in these towns is in the first and second centuries AD. In contrast, the evidence from the surrounding countryside suggests there was a significant rise in rural population which included new settlements in the steppe (ch. 4.4). Scores of villages are known of and many more lie beneath their modern counterparts. Overwhelmingly their dates – as measured by sherd scatters and by a handful of dated inscriptions – are of the late Roman/ early Umayyad period. As we have seen, some of these villages were really small towns. Even the much more modest new estimate for the population of Umm el-Jimal is still an impressive 2500-3000. Jimal is one of the largest, of course but there are other villages in the Southern Hauran which must certainly have had populations of a few hundred and occasionally more than 1000. Just *c.* 20 km northwest of Jimal is Umm es-Surab which, at *c.* 25 ha, is only a little smaller than Jimal. East of Jimal there are large ancient settlements within a few kilometres at Sabah, Dafyaneh and, in particular, Umm el-Quttein. The map (Fig. 5.1) tells the story with several dozen places seen by the Princeton Expedition a century ago and preserving usually significant traces of the 'Roman' period. They stretch north from Jimal to the fertile plain around Bostra and east from there to the big town of Salkhad. Including all the bigger places, the overall population could easily have been 25-30,000+ people.

With so little to go on, numbers are inevitably very imprecise and confidence in them cannot be high. They are individually often weak; collectively they are suggestive of smaller populations in cities than most modern commentators have believed. Rural population is impressive by ancient standards with, perhaps, 1000 villages and small towns in the region. Allowing *c.* 500 people in each as suggested for the limestone massif the rural population would be about 500,000.

Fig. 5.1. Roman villages in Southern Hauran, recorded by the Princeton Expedition.

5. Population and people

In short, a tentative suggestion would be:

Cities		Territory	
Average	Total	10%	20%
7,500-8000	c. 100,000	900,000	450,000

B. APPLICATION

Why do numbers matter? On the macro scale the considerations have already been alluded to (above). On the micro level of individual cities or the population of the region as a whole there are many obvious ways in which knowing something of numbers is illuminating. Only very occasionally do we have a piece of direct testimony for 'everyday life' in any of these Decapolis cities. Josephus' reference (*Bellum Judaicum* II.480) to the Jewish community at Gerasa in AD 66-70 is one such and references to various men of letters who originated at Gadara are another (Schürer 1979: 49). Let us explore one of the implications of the population numbers.

5.5. Cemeteries

The modern visitor to Decapolis cities and even to some of the ancient villages will often first confront the remains of cemeteries. Throughout the entire period of the LCM the traditional mode of disposing of the dead in this region was inhumation rather than cremation. In some cases there are above ground mausolea, sometimes the chambers for multiple burials were cut into the rock or into rock faces or utilized existing caves, sometimes just single slots cut in the rock. Other traces of cemeteries are stone sarcophagi and tombstones (usually in Greek but including many in Nabataean, a few in Latin and a growing corpus in Syro-Palestinian). The total evidence is considerable even on an impressionistic level – a few thousand identifiable tombs and graves, hundreds of epitaphs and several dozen sarcophagi. In reality it is a small part of what was once there.

Jones (1977: 20) suggests taking 25 per 1000 as a cautious estimate of mortality rates in a pre-industrial society. From that we may make a calculation for a medium-sized town like Gerasa with perhaps 10,000 inhabitants. Over the course of the first six centuries AD, when urbanization in the Decapolis was at its peak, Gerasa would have had c. 150,000 deaths (10 [thousands] x 25 [deaths per 1000] x 600 [years]). For the dozen cities of the region, if we average them at only 5000 people, then the total urban population would be c. 60,000. The total deaths then would be 900,000 (60 x 25 x 600). Add in the territory of each and the number soon amounts to several million even on the lowest population estimate of 300,000 overall (above). For the period of the LCM as a whole and for the entire 'virtual island', we may be dealing with the death and disposal of the remains of five or ten or even 20 million people. In a sense, which number is closest is unimportant. Even taking the lowest as a guide immediately reveals several factors of significance. First, where is the evidence for these dead? The number of graves identified (above) is a minute proportion of what might have been expected. Plainly the graves we see are those of the more prosperous inhabitants who could make provision for their decent disposal. Likewise, the few hundred tombstones we have must also be for the richer inhabitants. Conversely, the disposal of the vast majority of the dead in the cities of the region (and in the countryside as well) must have been far more informal; indeed, probably casual. We can only suppose that here, as in the imperial capital itself, the bodies of the dead were dumped in communal pits with minimal ceremony. The discovery of such communal graves at Rome in the nineteenth century was observed by Lanciani. He reported numerous pits, each about 5 x 4 x 10 m.

Closer to our region, we have some testimony in the sixth

5. Population and people

century AD 'Life of St Symeon the Fool'. After the saint's death at Emesa, we are told that he was buried 'in the place where strangers are buried' (Krueger 1996: 169-70). There is in fact no need to accumulate references. Disposal of the dead in any community was both an imperative and a routine matter. In light of the modest amount of evidence from every city of the region (and indeed from the empire as a whole), it is clear that most bodies must have been disposed of directly or indirectly by the agency of the local government and probably on middens or in communal pits. Among the Jews there were strict rules about burial places because of the fear of pollution, and a distance of 50 cubits (*c.* 25 m) from the settlement is mentioned. The other peoples of the Near East were probably as conscious of the contamination from burials. At a city such as Gerasa, a population of 10,000 would mean *c.* 250 deaths annually. In light of the relatively small number of formal tombs/ graves and markers, we may suppose the great majority of these dead were disposed of communally in pits. No such communal graves have been found at any of the cities or even the villages. Around a city such as Gerasa where might one logically and safely dispose of the physical remains of *c.* 150,000 dead? Aerial reconnaissance might reveal them.

6

A world of writing

And in order that the course of the proceedings as a whole may be more easily transmitted to the memory of future generations ... the senate has decided that the speech which our Princeps delivered and also these decrees of the senate, inscribed on bronze, should be set up in whatever place seems best to Ti. Caes(ar) Aug(ustus), and that likewise this decree of the senate, inscribed on bronze, should be set up in the most frequented city of each province and in the most frequented place in that city, and that likewise this decree of the senate, should be set up in the winter quarters of each legion where the standards are kept.

SC Gnaeus Piso, 10 December AD 20
(trans. M. Griffin, 'The Senate's Story',
JRS 87 [1997]: 253)

The Roman empire was bound together by writing. Literacy was both a social symbol and an integrative by-product of Roman government, economy, and culture. The whole experience of living in the Roman empire, of being ruled by Romans, was overdetermined by the existence of texts. I need hardly stress again that I am not arguing for near universal literacy; only a minority of Roman men could read and write. But the mass of literates, the density of their communications, and the volumes of their stored knowledge, significantly affected the experience of living in the Roman empire. Literacy and

6. A world of writing

writing were active ingredients in promoting cultural and ideological change.

Hopkins 1991: 144

6.1. Introduction

The Roman empire of the early centuries of our era was a 'world of writing'. Writing was to be seen everywhere and in numerous forms. More people were literate than ever before – or ever again for at least a thousand years. Writing was not just for the literate – it affected the lives of everyone in significant ways.

Writing most obviously can provide for the modern researcher details of people, places and events and even the small part that survives is a vital tool for explaining the nature of the ancient world and how it functioned. But writing was composed for the benefit of the ancients, not us: what was it for, who used it, what roles did it play both in the mundane world of the immediate (receipts, personal letters) and the longer term (as a store and transmitter of knowledge)? More than that, what role did it play in ordering and controlling lives, identifying and defining groups, *both literate and illiterate*. Finally, irrespective of its message, what role did it play as an *object*?

6.2. Writing in the Near East

Writing had a long history in the Near East – indeed, the beginnings of writing and cities are broadly contemporary in the mid-late fourth millennium BC. The rise of complex states stimulated the development of writing systems and the spread of such states across the Near East is marked by the parallel and rapid spread and usages of writing.

The major surviving evidence of writing in the pre-Classical Levant belongs to the late second and first millennium BC, but especially Iron Age II (beginning *c.* 900 BC). Writing materials are already varied – clay tablets, stone, plaster, ostraca, wood and wax tablets, skins, parchments and papyrus. Contracts, letters, receipts all become commoner, sacred texts are written down and disseminated. Probably of particular significance in the spread of writing was the need of the early empires for an administrative system and a method of communicating and organizing. The Persian empire evidently required sophisticated and elaborate writing systems whose growth and development stimulated private use, especially for contracts. Towards the end of the fifth century BC, both Persians and their Phoenician subjects started to use and inscribe coins. In addition to the archives of their predecessors, the Persians seem to have had libraries, too. Yet we should not exaggerate its significance. The examples are few in number and few people could read or would ever have seen writing; it played a small part in their lives (cf. Lewis 1994).

6.3. Greeks and Romans

Greek arrived in the Near East as a written language with the armies of Alexander in the late fourth century BC and the establishment of successor states; it was to displace local languages as the lingua franca for a millennium. Little survives in the region from the first three centuries. Papyri in Greek from Ptolemaic Egypt survive in its arid conditions and imply their existence in the Seleucid kingdom of Syria. Northwest Jordan lay between the two and was ruled by each in succession. No papyri survive there from this period but from Egypt comes the famous Zenon Archive of the third century BC whose documents relate to people in the region of Amman. They illustrate that letters, contracts and other documents were being written and regulating everyday life in one part of the Decapolis – as we would have guessed – and doubtless in them all. Egypt just happens to show us what was happening, perhaps on a larger

6. A world of writing

scale, elsewhere in the Levant with documents of all kinds, for archives and royal libraries.

All the Hellenistic rulers struck coins in large numbers and various denominations, bearing words as well as images. Some of the subject peoples of the wider area, such as the Phoenician states and Hasmonaean kingdom in Judaea, also struck coins.

With Rome there is a sharp increase in the surviving evidence. It has been calculated that for Egypt at least there was a twenty-fold increase in writing between the pharaonic period and the first two centuries AD (Hopkins 1991: 135; cf. Harris 1989: 276). Latin arrived as a written language in the mid-first century BC though it remained significantly less common than Greek everywhere except in the army camps. The examples cited in ch. 2 indicate the scale. There were other written languages. From NWJ there are Aramaic, Nabataean, several North Arabian languages (most notably 'Safaitic' – below), Syriac and even Melkite ('Syro-Palestinian') (cf. ch. 1.2).

In the cities, many inscriptions were cut on stone – on statue bases commemorating emperors, imperial officials and local worthies; religious dedications – altars to deities or commemoration of religious gifts; building inscriptions recording construction and its agents; public decrees; epitaphs on tombstones. Others were incised on metal, especially brass or bronze – most commonly public decrees. Graffiti are found scratched on stones or other material. Then there are texts painted on walls or stones and the inscriptions picked out in coloured stones in mosaics. The former belong to any period and are most commonly found on tomb walls; the latter are a late phenomenon, from after the heyday of stone inscriptions. Mosaics increasingly have words identifying figures, place-names beside stylised images of the place, and sometimes lengthy texts explaining the occasion on which a new floor was laid in a church, by whom and sometimes incorporating a religious tract.

Outside cities, inscriptions are still found widely. Tombstones are quite common in villages; other texts are associated with Roman military sites; and along the roads were erected milestones with quite lengthy, albeit formulaic inscriptions. And here and there were to be seen stones marking – with texts – the boundaries of estates or city territories. In one instance, in relation to Gerasa, at least ten markers were incised on the living rock – but at a scale and in places few would see except for shepherds or local landowners (Seigne 1997).

But these are the durable texts. Most writing then, as now, was on perishable material, mainly (in that region) papyrus but including significant numbers on skins, parchment or on waxed writing tablets. No single document on any one of these materials survives from NWJ but we can make useful inferences from the impressive and growing corpus of what has survived elsewhere in the Levant. Most famous are the parchments and papyri from the fortress city of Dura Europos on the middle Euphrates in eastern Syria (Welles et al. 1959). Largely of the late second and first half of the third century AD, some are civil documents recording contracts, loans and letters; most are military records revealing details of the everyday routines of the garrison from strength reports through leave requests to inventories. Even though related to a very short period and incomplete, they illustrate graphically just how much 'paperwork' was generated by the military, provide insights into its operation and also the extent to which written documents were a part of everyday life. Now we have a further selection of documents from northern Syria (Cotton, Cockle and Millar 1995).

Closer to home is the remarkable collection known as the Babatha Archive, described as constituting 'the single most precious repository of evidence that we have for private life and landholding in Roman Arabia and Palestine' (Bowersock 1991: 337). Babatha was a Jewess who evidently held on tightly to a sheaf of 37 documents relating to property, a loan contract,

6. A world of writing

legal matters concerning her children and in-laws and to her participation in the Roman census of AD 127. Babatha lived in Judaea/ Palaestina but owned property in the Nabataean kingdom. After AD 106 she dealt with the Roman authorities who had just taken over the kingdom and created the new province of Arabia. Most documents are in Greek but they include some Latin, Aramaic and Nabataean, sometimes in the same document (Lewis 1989). From nearby Masada the first century AD papyri add another type – inventories of (imported) foodstuffs (Cotton and Geiger 1989). And now we have the sixth century carbonised papyri from Petra (below).

There was an immense increase in the volume of coins in the Roman period and most were inscribed. Several of the Decapolis cities (including those in NWJ) struck their own coins for short periods (Spijkerman 1978) and the coins of other eastern mints were also in circulation. Most common, of course, were the imperial issues with their ever-changing images and words. Most economic activity undoubtedly remained one of barter and few people raised themselves much above a subsistence level. Nevertheless, coinage was abundant and its texts found their way into every hand.

6.4. The scale of writing

One recent scholar has argued that in the cities of the empire within a short time the public places would have been festooned with examples of writing (Ando 2000: ch. 4). By the third century AD the agora of even the small cities of NWJ would have had dozens of texts – statue bases, altars, decrees, building records; texts were inscribed on buildings and even (including Gerasa) on columns on the main streets. Far more significant were texts on perishable materials. The recent tabulation of 'papyrological' items (including wood and ostraca) from the Near East outside Egypt, runs to over 600 items and is highly suggestive that the range and scale was comparable to that of Egypt (Cotton, Cockle and Millar 1995).

Official documents and archives

It is likely the traveller in, say, Gerasa would see numerous examples of letters posted publicly and including some such statement by the official who originated them as 'Let each of you take care that a copy of this letter is displayed publicly in the district-capitals and in every village in clear and easily legible writing on a whitened board ...' (*P.Oxy.* XXXIV: 2705, 10-12 quoted in Bowman 1991: 121; cf. Ando 2000: 96-101). Indeed, we now have a document from Arabia showing how even a census declaration of property was publicly displayed (at Rabbathmoab in Central Jordan):

> Verified exact copy of a document of registration which is displayed in the basilica here ... (*P.Yadin* 16).

The state not only issued instructions and edicts intended for widespread display in cities, towns and villages but set a date at which the display would commence uniformly and the duration so as to allow the community to view the item (Ando 2000: 98-101).

But beyond the fluttering public letters was the largely unseen writing. One or more of the public buildings would have housed the city archives – the city's constitution, the minutes of meetings of the council, the records of imperial or gubernatorial decisions, manumission records, copies of at least some petitions, records of land holdings (manuals imply the widespread existence of such material) and census and tax records (Ando 2000: ch. 4; cf. Isaac 1996). The keeping of official archives was a mark of a complex civilized society – writing about the eastern Roman empire, the Chinese source called the Wei-Lo – perhaps

6. A world of writing

derived from an embassy of AD 97, says flatly and significantly, 'they have official archives' (Hirth 1885: 70; Wei-Lo 35).

For Arabia, once again we can turn to the Babatha Archive, which explicitly tells us:

> Verified exact copy of one item from the minutes of the council of Petra the metropolis, minutes displayed in the temple of Aphrodite in Petra, ... (*P.Yadin* 12).

Though hidden from view, these in particular were the texts which most 'entangled' people. They ordered, controlled and defined the lives of individuals in a meaningful and everyday fashion. More than that, their very existence gave a depth to the history of the community: the stored memories of people and events whether the decrees of emperors or the census declarations of small farmers. As Eck observed (2002: 155), publicly displayed inscriptions were 'intended to create a collective memory'. If they were there they played a role; if they were not the information such texts might contain did not exist.

It is worth underscoring just how common were the official documents of the Roman world. Ando (2000: 80-96) has reminded us how common it was for the Roman state to correspond with communities throughout the empire and to supply them with documents or request copies from *their* archives. Such documents were often vital for establishing the status and rights of communities. As for the mundane, the Babatha Archive is highly instructive (above). And now for the sixth century AD we have the *c.* 50 documents found carbonised in a burnt church at Petra. Once again their significance lies not just in specific details of 'dowry settlements, resolutions of disputes, sworn agreements to property divisions and exchanges, registrations of property sales, transfers of tax responsibilities and receipts for payments of civic and military taxes' (Taylor 2002: 208), but in general the very mundane

Gerasa and the Decapolis

material committed to paper by people of modest means. One document is 8-9 metres in length and bears 600-700 lines of text – all this recording the settlement of a land dispute in the village of Zadocatha, 30 km south of Petra (Koenen and Kaimio 1997).

The number of such documents known from even the wider region of Arabia or Syria is pathetically small (cf. 2.1). In relation to Egypt, Hopkins has made a useful calculation about the survival rate of just one type of document – census returns (see ch. 7.4) (1991: 133n.2). We may apply the same calculation to NWJ between 106 and the same terminal date of 257, with a 14-year census cycle, family sizes averaging five people and a population of no more than *c.* 500,000. The ten censuses would produce 100,000 census returns per census and a million over the period. In practice, the Babatha Archive gives us our *sole* example for the entire province. If we take just Gerasa and assume 10,000 people in the town and a further 40,000 in the territory, we would expect 10,000 per census and 100,000 examples overall.

We may take, too, the case of the loyalty *libelli*. In a remarkable episode, the Emperor Decius required *everyone* to prove their pagan status by making a public sacrifice and libation and receiving a *libellus* in proof. More than 50 are known, all so far from Egypt all dating to between 2 June and 14 July 250. We have none for the entire Near East. Likewise for the Near East we have none of the petitions that survive in large numbers in Egypt and about which we hear enough in ancient literary sources to suggest they were generated in the tens of thousands annually (Hopkins 1991: 137). But we can be confident they existed in NWJ, too.

Private documents

Then there were the private, informal documents. A Dura papyrus listing items for a temple explicitly includes paper. We know it was common at shrines for visitors to post documents.

6. A world of writing

Despite the likely variation between shrines, Beard (1991: 39-44) insists that the evidence we have is clear: shrines and temples were often awash in writing – scraps of paper, wax tablets, graffiti, painted texts, formal inscribed dedications, offering vows, thanks, requests etc. She reminds us of a passage in Juvenal (*Satires* XII.98f.):

> But if some wealthy/ spinster or bachelor catches the mildest fever, you'll find/ the whole of the temple cloisters [= portico] soon hung with votive prayers/ for the invalid's speedy recovery.

We have no such evidence from the Decapolis but we have the abundant evidence from other places, including the East (e.g. Pergamum in Asia and Talmis in southern Egypt). Most is of course perishable though the numerous curses inscribed on lead in western provinces points to another form we should be alert for. The cleaning of the pool at Bath in Britain revealed 130 inscribed lead curse tablets. They evidently existed in the Near East as well – Tacitus speaks of 'spells, curses, lead tablets inscribed with the patient's name' at Antioch in AD 18 (*Annals* 2.69).

In the towns were guilds and trade associations of the type attested in Gerasa for linen-weavers and potters. Such organizations elsewhere – and doubtless in the Decapolis, too – developed written rules and maintained records of their proceedings. This is not just a matter of more texts. As Hopkins observes (1991: 155) 'written rules surely defined obligations rather more rigidly and more fixedly than purely oral agreements'. The same would have been true of many of the pagan cults.

Examples like these make clear that paperwork was generated in staggering quantities and was often of importance to the individuals concerned, much of it bringing the presence and weight of the state into their lives. Privately, too, people generated a mass of texts. Equally it is clear that almost all of this paperwork, many millions of items, has been lost, mostly irrevocably.

On view

A traveller in northern Jordan, arriving from the east in, say, AD 250, would find at camping places in the Basalt Desert rock art and dozens of short inscriptions in 'Safaitic' and would be told of their abundance throughout the region (below). Along the simple desert roads he could see at regular intervals the short basalt milestones inscribed in Latin with a Latin and Greek numeral for distance and commemorating the work of the emperors of 40 years before. In the pre-desert and settled areas the milestones were tall limestone columns and by the mid-third century, individual mile-stations might have multiple stones standing like sentinels at the roadside, all again in Latin, and perhaps letters picked out in red paint. Now, as farmlands appeared, the traveller would encounter the occasional boundary marker in Latin or Greek. Military posts were strung out at intervals and the main forts at least would commonly have a prominent inscription, usually in Latin, recording its building history. The troops themselves included a high proportion who were literate (Harris 1989: 253-5) and able to maintain the mass of everyday paperwork in their camps: some maintained strength reports and duty rosters, others drafted letters granting leave or giving specific instructions; some consulted the military calendar to check what imperial event of the past two and a half centuries required commemoration and the appropriate sacrifice that day (*P.Dura* 54). Everyday transactions with the military would place a premium on literacy. Inscribed coins would be in frequent use in the civil settlements around the forts and here or at other points along the route, the traveller might have to pay one for customs duty or a bridge toll for both of which a receipt would be issued.

6. A world of writing

As the traveller approached each village he might see a scatter of simple epitaphs inscribed and/ or painted on stone and perhaps wooden boards, perhaps even an imperial judgement on a monumental block. A locally significant shrine might be festooned with prayers scribbled on 'paper'.

At the first major city the cemeteries lined the approach roads outside the walls and if it was only a minority who erected epitaphs, still the effect of dozens of epitaphs would be considerable. The city gate itself would likely be marked by a monumental inscription in Latin or Greek picked out in blood-red letters. Along the streets our traveller would see shop signs and graffiti on house walls and inscriptions cut on columns recording the individuals or guilds of workers who had donated the item generations before. As public buildings came into view the numbers of texts increased. Altars by the dozen stood in the precincts in front of the great temples obscuring the building inscriptions. On the very walls would be inscribed texts about the affairs of the community – some directly on the building stone, some on attached stones (often of marble), some on impressive bronze, brass or copper tablets. In and around the agora stood scores of statues; emperors of every period, all named on the plinths on which their image stood. Inside the municipal buildings would be yet more inscribed texts – building records in some, the names of voting tribes cut on the seats in the theatre, religious dedications, decrees concerning government and law.

And if the traveller ventured into an archive building or the part of a temple used for them, he would have confronted mounds of documents accumulated over generations and still being added to. But on a modest scale, surely every house contained a few simple pieces of writing, the personal archives of peasant or lord for everything from tax through census to property ownership.

6.5. Visibility and use

For whom were these texts important? Who could read them? Did they matter to any but the few who could read them or the still smaller numbers to whom they related?

It has been estimated (Harris 1989: 272) that at its peak probably less than 5-10% of the population in the western provinces was literate. The East had longer traditions and higher levels. If it had reached only 10% that would still mean a hefty one and half to two million *could* read in the East alone (cf. Hopkins 1991: 134-5) and they tended to be concentrated in towns and military camps. Indeed, the proliferation and growth of towns stimulated literacy. Moreover, as Bowman observes of the public letters of Egypt, they only make sense if their content could be known to everyone – 'inability to read would not have been accepted as a legitimate excuse for ignorance' (1991: 121-2; cf. Ando 2000: 96-103). People were expected to know the content of official letters that had a bearing on their lives and conduct. Bowman again: 'it can only mean that those who could not read (or write) participated in literacy in some significant way' and in a passage of Justinian's *Digest* the jurist Ulpian, speaking of the public display of documents, asks:

> Should it be written in Greek, or in Latin? I think that depends on the location, lest someone be able to plead ignorance of the letters. Certainly, if someone should say that he didn't understand the letters or did not see what was posted, when many did read and the notice was publicly posted, then he will not be heard (*Digest* 14.3.11.3 quoted in Ando 2000: 98).

Obvious examples of imperial or gubernatorial announcements people were required to know about would be registration at the periodic census and to ensure that records of tax payments were

6. A world of writing

made and accurate. We may suppose, too, that edicts announced the timing and places of the annual assize circuit. But Ando (2000: 73-80) has gone further and argued that writing was more than merely useful. Rather, it was part of a contract between state and subject. The former proclaimed its virtues and good intentions and that required them then to advertise and explain what it was doing and to make it possible for the latter to know about these and enter into the consensus that made the empire attractive or at least tolerable and diminished the need for force.

In a world in which writing was so common and of such significance, there would have been an impetus to acquire some reading skill and/ or routinely to seek explanations from those who were literate. Not just for the plainly important items (tax receipts, loan contracts, etc.); we may infer a population which clearly understood the importance of writing in their everyday lives and routinely sought explanations of public writing. In short even the peasant taking produce to market or travelling further to an assize centre, would have viewed the milestones passed as more than mere objects. The frequency with which Eusebius in his *Onomasticon* locates places by reference to a numbered milestone (Freeman-Grenville, Chapman and Taylor 2003: 175-84) makes it certain travellers measured distances by counting them. They may also have been conscious of what the milestones said.

The significance of writing can be seen in another way. Many publicly displayed texts in the communities of the empire explicitly record that they are an extract of an original on display at a named location in Rome itself (Ando 2000; 80-90 for examples). One group who would have been especially conscious of this fact are locally settled veteran soldiers. Even those who had scant knowledge of writing would have kept carefully the record of their discharge which detailed their privileges. The best known examples are the bronze tablets scholars call 'diplomas'. The soldier would certainly know what the diploma actually said and could probably identify the key elements. More than that, they would know it was an extract, a copy from the original inscribed on the wall of a named public building in the imperial capital. E.g.

> Recorded and authorized from the bronze plaque which is affixed at Rome on the Capitoline on the left side of the Public Record Office (Roxan *RMD* I: no. 3).

Some documents named public buildings closer to home – Babatha's census return explicitly informs the reader that the original was in the minutes of the Temple of Aphrodite at Petra (*P.Yadin* 12) (above).

From such documents, not just the veteran but many others would be conscious they inhabited a world defined by writing. The documents would simultaneously control their lives and reveal the scale of the world in which they lived. Distant places – even Rome itself – would be named and have significance. Their world would be enlarged by writing but distances would be shrunk through an increased familiarity. The world beyond their own community would seem less alien and more accessible. Indeed, it may be that in creating a wider but seemingly smaller world, writing also made one's own community seem smaller and more parochial. Not just those with Roman citizenship but many others might feel more a part of something large, extending well beyond their immediate community. Examples of imperial edicts erected in villages in the Hauran underscore that the emperor and his involvement in your life could reach into the smaller units in the most remote places (e.g. Oliver 1974; Roussel and Visscher 1942-43).

But many people were more than just functionally literate. The Decapolis cities – especially Gadara and Gerasa – produced notable men in various branches of learning: philosophers,

6. A world of writing

poets, rhetoricians and, most famously, the historian Nicolaus of Damascus (Schürer 1979: II, 49). We may readily assume that the elites of the cities were not just literate but familiar with the literature of their culture. For the Jews among them that literature included a religious text that provided both a living guide for regulating their everyday conduct and a record of the depth of their history and their place in the world (Millar 1993: 337-41). This sacred text was almost unique in the Levant. The exception is Christianity which drew on the Hebrew Bible and developed it with its own additional books. The spread of Christianity and its own appetite for writing go hand in hand with the transition from the roll text to the codex whose form proved far more useful for consultation and storage.

No matter what their ethnic origin, however, or religious belief, the educated people of NWJ shared a Graeco-Roman culture and the literature that was a common stock for them all. The elites of the Roman Decapolis cities would be familiar with the great works of Classical Greece and the writings of at least those Romans who wrote in Greek. Many may well have been familiar with not just Polybius and Cassius Dio but Cicero, Caesar and Tacitus. Even those who could not read the Latin of Pliny the Elder could read the Greek of Strabo's *Geography* and the technical treatises which explained and gave meaning (however inaccurate) to their world. The Augustan period and first century AD was a time in which a succession of writers described and explained the natural world in which they lived. Peoples and places, things living and inert, phenomena, were all dealt with. Maps were drawn and put on display. Expeditions (the Yemen) and journeys of exploration (down the Nile) were carried out. Trade contacts introduced a familiarity with distant places and people (East Africa, India). The very act of writing it down, too, defined and ordered and controlled their world, made it smaller, more manageable, less frightening and gave people increased confidence. It also created a sharper sense of Us (the civilized people of the Roman world) and Them (the strange people outside) but stimulated the latter to emulate Us (cf. ch. 6.6).

The Near East is a polyglot region and it was not enough to know one's own language even if one was literate in it. As the Babatha Archive reveals, everyday transactions could be conducted and recorded in multiple languages. Not just the various Aramaic and proto-Arabic dialects of the region but the Greek of much official business and later the Latin of the imperial power. People did not just hear different languages around them but would see them, too. Nabataean on coins, the proto-Arabic of 'Safaitic' graffiti, 'Melkite' on tombstones and mosaics, Latin on milestones and military texts and Greek everywhere.

One explanation for the spread of literacy is simply its usefulness. As Goody observed (1968: 1-2), writing enables 'speech [to] ... be transmitted over space and preserved over time'. But there are other explanations which can shed light on how writing functioned in northern Jordan. Writing confers status. Being able to read unlocks information and gives the power to share or not share that information with others. Conversely, not being able to read in a world increasingly penetrated by writing is weakening and the custodians of literacy can become oppressive to the illiterate. Being able to read enabled one to confront those with custody of texts and exploit the certainty of written records for one's own ends.

Finally, the sheer bulk of writing, whatever its precise content, is testimony to the penetration of the Roman state in particular and the role it was felt to play in creating unity. As McKitterick (1990: 324) has observed in another context:

> The use of the written word gave the Carolingian empire unity; the elite of the Carolingian world actively participated in literacy as a means of group identification, for their own benefit; hence, as Nelson pointed out, the 'effec-

6. A world of writing

tiveness' of literacy in government should be appreciated as much for its symbolic as for its pragmatic function. ... (a government's) assumption of the value of literacy and exploitation of literate modes has much to tell us of the literate mentalities of that society as a whole.

6.6. 'Safaitic' inscriptions

To date some 30,000 are known (with scores of thousands more inferred), two-thirds of them from northern Jordan, most of the rest from neighbouring southern Syria. The likely total is large – perhaps double or treble the number recorded. Spread over, say, four centuries, this represents about 75 a year on average, but potentially 150-200 if we include those not yet recorded. Even today, when human numbers have risen sharply, this region of Jordan has a population of only *c.* 16,000 (Dutton et al. 1998: 219).

One of the few authorities on the material has acutely observed that examples are seldom found in villages but overwhelmingly in desert areas (Macdonald 1993: 311-13). They are not the work of sedentarists but of nomads, a group whose reputation for oral transmission is fabled and who might seem additionally disinclined to need writing. The graffiti might still only be the work of a minority but overall that may be broadly comparable to the extent of writing as a skill among their sedentary cousins.

Why did nomads in the Basalt Desert areas acquire at least rudimentary writing skills? Until recently, their descendants were almost entirely illiterate yet these ancient peoples could inscribe names, genealogies, places, and sometimes record brief events, all of it in a writing peculiar to themselves. The texts are simple – 'boasts, laments, prayers together with genealogies' – and are often accompanied by simple pictures of people and animals. The texts and even the words are written left to right, top to bottom and their reverses, in a circle and even upside down; sometimes more than one form in the same text or on the same stone. Almost frivolous, game-playing. He infers, too, that the writing was developed for use on stone and was not the outgrowth of an existing cursive form used on soft materials. They are, he concludes, 'a form of self-expression rather than communication' (Macdonald 1993: 388; cf. *ABD* 3: 420). He goes on to argue that these people developed writing and this form of expression because they could do so easily and then use it as a simple but attractive time-filler in a society in which boredom was a feature. 'It must thus have come to be used as a pastime, something to do while engaged in pasturing the animals or keeping watch, occupations very often mentioned in the texts and ones in which time often hangs heavy' (Macdonald 1993: 386).

Can we go further? The texts are thought to extend from the first century BC to the fourth century AD. This is the very period which saw the growth of Nabataean power in the Hauran and the arrival of Rome in the region, her control of the settled land and expanding influence over cross-desert trade routes, and gradual penetration of the pre-desert and desert. It is the period, too, of the explosion of writing in her domain in the forms described above. The nomads lived in an area which, through transhumance, took them from winter pasturage in the desert (largely outside direct Roman control till the third century AD) to summer pasturage within the directly administered lands and a symbiotic relationship with the farmer who could employ their labour and animals and engage in simple trade. Although drawing and writing may well have been agreeable time-fillers there are other possibilities:

> ... because of the nomadic character of the peoples in question, graffiti acquired among them a surprisingly wide range of functions. Circumstances encouraged them

6. A world of writing

to leave written messages in order to maintain contact with each other and to establish rights to wells and camping sites (Harris 1989: 189n.79).

Safaitic inscriptions may be more significant for their existence and location than for what they say. They were the nomad's counterpart to the Graeco-Roman practice of labelling roads, setting up territorial markers, and making maps of possessions.

More than that, were 'Safaitic' inscriptions a reaction to the appearance and spread of writing among the Nabataeans and later the subjects of the great power on their doorstep and with whom they engaged? A 'technology of power' (Moreland 2001: 88) stimulated by or in reaction to the quite rapid development of writing as an instrument of control and form of display in the settled lands of northern Jordan? In short, was it a primitive form of emulation on one level and also, on another, an assertion of equality with the agents of imperial power and even, paradoxically, a claim to being civilized, too? The relationship could be emulation by an ally or friend or even by an enemy (as the nomads certainly could be at times).

The character of the texts may also be instructive. Overwhelmingly they are genealogies, some going back ten or even 15 generations. They may be boasting but perhaps also suggest possession of the land and stress the antiquity of that. With very few exceptions, however, these thousands of texts have nothing to say of the outside world – rather, these people are intensely introverted and use their skill to record very mundane matters (cf. Sartre 2005: 234-7).

Why did the inscribers of 'Safaitic' texts stop producing them? Perhaps they didn't – or rather, perhaps they shifted to something else. As noted, these texts ended in the third or fourth century. Is it simple coincidence that it is at this time that Roman penetration of the pre-desert and Basalt Desert is powerfully under way? A Roman road with milestones dated to 208/10 was constructed into the Azraq Oasis and inscriptions reveal the building of a fort – perhaps two (ch. 4). Other inscriptions and excavation reveal a growing military involvement in the third and fourth centuries and especially around *c.* AD 300 (Kennedy 2004b: chs 7-8; cf. 9). It is at this same time that the evidence for the growth of villages in the pre-desert, especially the Southern Hauran, strengthens. The settlements are not necessarily new but their growth into villages or even small towns is the striking feature of the period (ch. 4).

These villages are largely late Roman in date – even if they often overlie earlier settlement of some kind, their development into permanent stone-built villages was largely the work of the fourth to seventh centuries. Another feature of many of these places is the commonness of inscriptions. In part, of course, that may be simply that the remoteness of these places has taken a lesser toll of the remains even in comparison with cities like Gerasa. Even if disproportionately preserved through accident, the fact remains that there are often large numbers of inscriptions in these villages. At Umm el-Jimal the latest count is of almost 500 inscriptions in several ancient languages. But even in smaller places there can be remarkably large numbers. At Umm el-Quttein there are 40: a Latin military inscription from the village and another from a nearby hill, both probably of the second century AD; several milestones in Latin, some brought into the village from the roads themselves and all dated to AD 293-324; nine in Nabataean, almost all funerary; the remainder (23) in Greek and almost all epitaphs.

Much may be learned from what these texts say. A name and the patronymic are commonly Semitic and ages at death are almost invariably divisible by five or ten implying ignorance of the actual age: e.g. 'Bannathe (the daughter) of Omethos, age 25' (MacAdam and Graf 1989: 178). For present purposes, however, what is of interest is the fact of quite numerous

6. A world of writing

though simple epitaphs cut on slabs of basalt and apparently belonging to the late Roman period. In contrast, tombstones from the much larger cities are surprisingly rare and, if scarcely less informative, are generally better cut, perhaps professionally, and often of the early Roman period. In short, at about the time the inscribing of 'Safaitic' became less common then disappeared entirely, and epitaphs became scarce in cities, the inhabitants of the pre-desert and Hauranic villages, start setting up inscriptions and especially tombstones in large numbers. Evidently the practice is not new – numerous Nabataean texts including epitaphs are known from, probably, the first century AD. But there is a transition to Greek as the medium and the numbers grow along with the settlements themselves. There is a problem being certain who the inhabitants of these villages were (ch. 4). The best guess is that they are sedentarized nomads. In short we may be witnessing the settlement – presumably voluntary – of people who had developed their own script for thousands of graffiti and are now adopting Greek like their new neighbours. Many 'Safaitic' texts were, of course, funerary and found precisely on cairns heaped over bodies.

6.7. Conclusion

The impression one gets from a visit today to any Roman urban or military site and even from many villages is of a time and place in which writing was prominent. The impression is misleading in that it so dramatically underestimates the scale and importance of writing to people at the time – *all* the people, both literate and illiterate. The accident of survival (Egypt, Pompeii, graffiti in desert areas) or the chance of discovery (Dura Europos, the Babatha Archive, the Petra Papyri) in even a tiny handful of places give insights into the range and scale of the loss. We need not doubt its existence, however; we may never have a single piece of writing on a perishable material (papyrus, skin, wood) from Jordan but can be quite certain they were generated and existed there in the millions over the course of the Graeco-Roman period in particular. Throughout that period but especially in the Roman centuries, the significance of writing in the lives of the population would have been immense in every way from the mundane (receipts for the illiterate) through the creation for the literate of a 'private mental world' (Harris 1989: 126) to texts which conveyed authority even to those who could not read.

Yet an assessment of writing cannot be just about what has survived or even of what was once there. The disappearance of writing from where it once existed, the absence of writing in particular places or contexts, shifts in the types of writing and the very fact of the invention of writing systems for local dialects all have something to tell us.

The number of literates was large but it was uneven in time and place. For example, women everywhere were far less likely to be literate. The decline in literary texts in the fourth century AD has been seen as 'a symptom of and a cause of a profound cultural change, an extensive loss of awareness of past achievements in history-writing, in philosophy, in all genres of imaginative literature, and eventually in mathematics'. But alongside that we find the growth of hagiographical writing and the development of the codex book. Coptic and Syriac have been seen as languages invented as forms of resistance to the power of the Roman state (Harris 1989: 146-7); perhaps so, too, was 'Safaitic'. The widespread use of writing on tombstones especially in the third century and its virtual disappearance thereafter is striking but then we have dozens of dated epitaphs of the fifth to early seventh centuries in Moab (Canova 1954). Then there is the collapse of documentation for the Roman army in the crisis of the mid-third century, its revival under the Tetrarchs at the end of the century then huge shrinkage in the subsequent centuries. Euse-

6. A world of writing

bius' repeated location of places in relation to named milestones underscores how useful they remained. Yet they were routinely and frequently set up for two or three centuries and then the practice ceased entirely both for repairs and new roads. Why? Fashion? Transfer of the task of maintenance from state to local authority? A shift to pack roads instead of wheeled ones?

In the fourth century the level of state writing seems to decline and a great deal of private inscribing disappears. But new modes of writing appear. Church mosaics frequently include texts, sometimes extensive. Copies of the sacred text of the newly state-sponsored religion become commoner but so, too, do commentaries on it with 'new literate groups and new uses of writing' (Harris 1989: 285).

We can also make plausible estimates of the level literacy reached and the extent to which an even wider circle could read and understand or have access to the content of texts. The growth of many villages and towns and the impressive numbers of cities, gave a density to writing that surely played a role in stimulating it further and enhancing its significance. The scores of epitaphs from each of the little villages of the Hauran, for example, are poor sources of direct evidence beyond names and guesses at age. But what is surely equally if not more interesting is that so many people who were probably sedentarized nomads chose to start marking graves with texts and to use Greek. What did it mean to the inhabitants of a little place like the Roman village at Umm el-Quttein to see dozens of Greek epitaphs in the cemeteries of the community?

Writing of the early Middle Ages in northwestern Europe, McKitterick (1990: 320; cf. 5) sums it up well:

> [Literacy] was not only a quantitative matter of who could read and write, and a kind of technology. It was also a mentality, a form of ideology through which power could

be exerted, a frame of mind and a framer of minds; it was both the consequence of, and had as a consequence, particular kinds of social practice.

Despite the scale of usage we must end this survey with the reminder that even at its height, the ancient world was still overwhelmingly an oral one. Not just in the obvious sense that most people were illiterate and transacted their business and conducted their lives orally. Even the state played its role with the provision for the oral presentation of information – heralds making announcements and newly posted documents of the state being read out as well as displayed. Nor should we forget the importance of visual messages, which were so vital in communicating with the illiterate (cf. Brown 1999).

7

The structures of the Roman state

> ... the material culture of the Incas, their roads, buildings, and artefacts were, on the surface at least, more accessible to sixteenth century beholders than the principles of political and social order that held the empire together.
>
> MacCormack 2001: 419

7.1. The provinces

Historians devote a great deal of time and effort to defining the location, size and shape of individual Roman provinces; to identifying the status and terms of office of provincial governors; and to determining the administrative arrangements within provinces. Many archaeologists may feel it is of no interest to them, being about politics and government. That is surely wrong and we must turn to what we know of Roman provincial administration to illustrate why the location of a city or town or community in one province rather than another mattered to the way in which it developed and can be central to interpretation of the archaeological remains.

Numbers and size

The Roman empire was divided into provinces. The number varied. In about 120 AD there were some 40 provinces; in 300 AD over much the same area there were more than 100. It is unlikely we would know that but for written sources. In other words, the early Roman empire had provinces that were large by historic standards – for example, Britannia, comprising all of modern England, Wales and parts of Scotland, was a single unit. Later, however, Britannia was divided into two provinces, then into four. Arabia, too, was modified and divided. The size of administrative unit matters as it tells us something about the ratio of elite administrators to population. In the case of Rome we can see the ratio is very high and compares highly unfavourably with twelfth-century southern China (Hopkins 1980: 120-1).

Boundaries

Written sources also provide clues to the location of provincial boundaries and to changes that occurred from time to time. What would archaeologists infer? In the southern part of the Near East, geography suggests the broad divisions administration *might* favour (ch. 3). The great trough of the rift valley stands out, running from the Sea of Galilee as far at the Gulf of Aqaba, plunging to 200 m below sea level and flanked by hills and plateau on either side. It is the boundary between states today. East of the Jordan, the lateral cuts of the Wadi Yarmuk in the north suggest a possible point of division while further south the deep and penetrating valleys of the Wadi Mujib and Wadi al-Hasa are effective separators of communities to this day. In short, without texts one might suppose an administrative unit east of the rift valley to have been bounded by it with one or more sub-division created by the great east-west valleys.

Written sources reveal a surprising reality (Figs 7.1a and b). First, in the pre-Roman period, parts of NWJ had at various times been ruled from *west* of the Jordan and that continued in Roman times. Herod the Great and his successors ruled a region called the Peraea east of the Jordan (as well as the Gaulanitis, Batanea, Trachonitis and Auranitis reaching far to

7. The structures of the Roman state

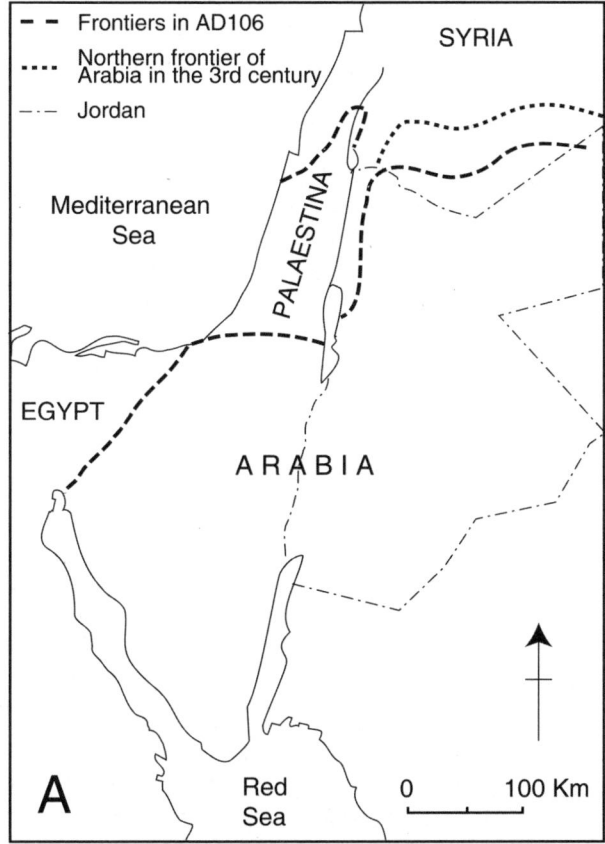

Fig. 7.1a and b (*overleaf*). The changing administrative boundaries of the southern Near East in the Roman period (from Kennedy 2004b: 41).

the east of the Sea of Galilee). The Roman province of Judaea which emerged in the early/ mid-first century AD and replaced the Herodian principalities, included the Peraea and some cities of the Decapolis in Transjordan. Historically the Greek Decapolis cities of NWJ passed under Roman control in 63 BC and were part of the province of Syria governed from Antioch far to the north. But a further twist was the temporary attach-

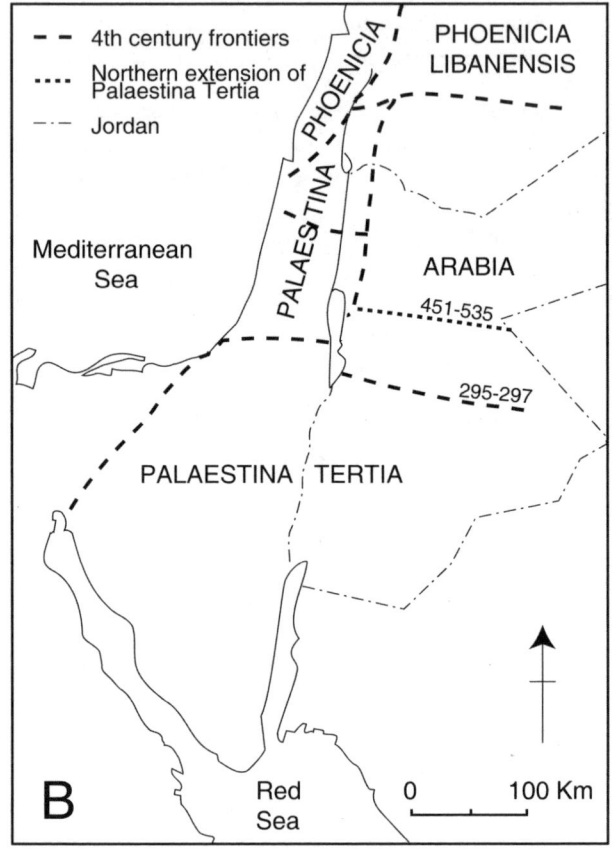

ment of at least one of those cities – Gadara – to Herod's kingdom. As we now know, however, from an inscription, the Romans themselves acknowledged the administrative awkwardness of this arrangement and delegated everyday administrative control of the Decapolis to an equestrian officer (prefect) responsible to the governor (Isaac 1981 [= 1998: ch. 20]).

In AD 106 the Nabataean kingdom was annexed by Rome (Fig. 7.2). It had stretched from the northern Hedjaz on the east side of the Gulf of Aqaba, through the Hisma and Negev De-

7. The structures of the Roman state

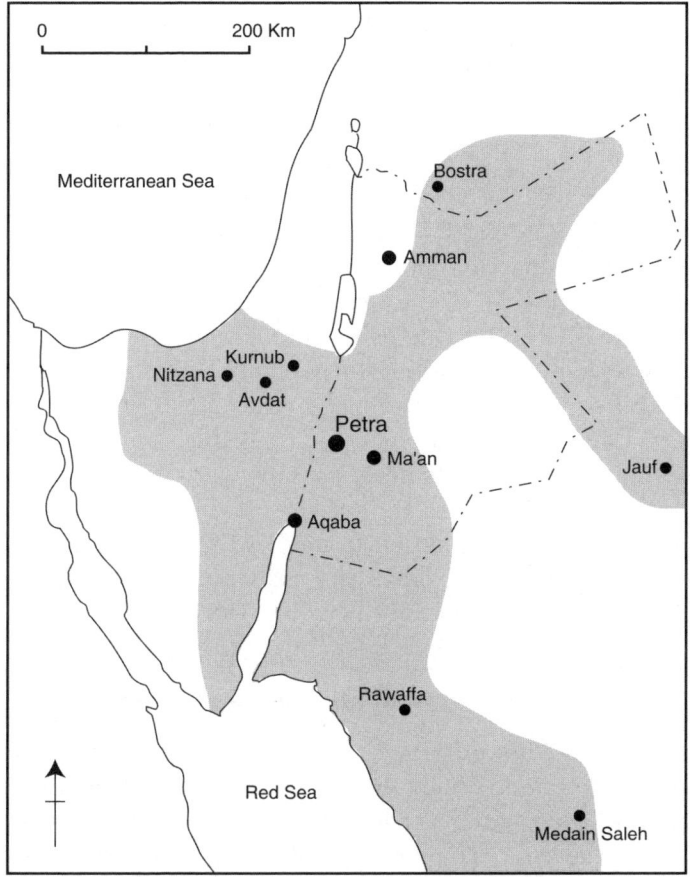

Fig. 7.2. The Nabataean kingdom (from Kennedy 2004: 38).

serts, the plateau of Edom where Petra itself lay, through Moab and in an arc northeastwards around the Decapolis to the Southern Hauran and the flourishing city of Bostra. The new province is unexpected. First, the seat of the governor was shifted from Petra to Bostra far to the north where a legion of c. 5000 Roman citizen soldiers was headquartered (though numerous detachments seem to have been outposted across the entire province). In short, instead of an administrative location central to the province, one more suited to wider imperial considerations was chosen. At the same time some of the cities of the Decapolis – Philadelphia and Gerasa, and probably Adraha – were detached from the province of Syria and added to Arabia. Apparently now or soon afterwards – the evidence is unclear – Gadara and Pella were also detached from Syria and attached to Palaestina along with Scythopolis, the only Decapolis city that side of the Jordan. Capitolias and Abila are difficult to allocate at this point but were certainly not part of Arabia. At a later date when the northern boundaries of Arabia were shifted, one of the Decapolis cities north of the Yarmuk River – Canatha – was transferred to Arabia.

Administratively, therefore, not only were the Decapolis cities split between no less than three provinces but even those lying in the geographical unit formed by the Highlands of Ajlun were split between at least two provinces and involved an unexpected spanning of the rift valley. Does it matter?

7.2. Provincial governors at work

As Ando (2000) has observed, much that we know the state did is seldom attested. Fragments of evidence reveal the ubiquity of such things as rituals of loyalty to the dynasty or the public posting of decrees. The routines of officials emerge here and there and are evidently common across the empire or large parts of it for generations.

Although the evidence is very limited and fragmented, it combines to underscore that for the period of the early empire at least, there were broad similarities. If one approaches these similarities cautiously and avoids insisting on exact replication, much may be inferred with confidence about how the Roman state *must* have operated on an everyday basis in NWJ and what the significance was.

7. The structures of the Roman state

Arriving and departing

Not just the emperors, but the Roman aristocracy in general operated in a predictable and formal fashion in their official duties. The departure from or return to Rome of the emperor was formulaic, recorded on coins proclaiming Arrival/ Departure and is a common motif in relief sculpture on imperial monuments. It involved official greetings by the aristocracy and crowds meeting him well beyond the city, sometimes with seating provided to present a pageant for the imperial party. Likewise emperors were publicly greeted and seen off at cities they visited. On a more modest scale a governor was similarly treated. Here I want to look at the related question of *where* the governors of Arabia entered and left their province. This is a significant matter. Beyond the pageantry and colour of the occasion it involved honour and status for the community/ies in general. It also gave the local elite an opportunity to make contact with this senior Roman senator and establish a relationship that might be vital to their well-being during his tenure of office. It involved expense, too, as the governor and his entourage had to be housed, fed and entertained. And because of the regularity of the event their city itself might develop in a way that reflected their regular role in welcoming and farewelling the governor.

Beginning in AD 106 governors of Arabia began to arrive and depart regularly, at intervals of about two to three years. How would a new governor reach Bostra or return to Rome? There is no explicit evidence for Arabia, but the character and pattern of such arrivals/ departures can be gleaned from other places. The evidence empire-wide is thin but consistent, although we may suppose there was variation and no rigidly prescribed rule. For Asia, as late as the early second century AD, a newly appointed governor still had some discretion, but by the time the Digest was compiled, the point of entry had long been fixed at Ephesus. Certainly even Pliny the Younger en route to Bithynia reports (Pliny *Epistulae* 10.15 [cf. 17a]) that he intends to sail on to there from Ephesus, and Hadrian entered Asia at that city:

> Emperor Caesar Traianus Hadrianus Augustus, ... Tribunician Power XIII [= AD 129], Consul III, Father of his Country: 'To the Chief Magistrates, Council and People of Ephesus, greetings. Lucius Erastos tells me that he is a citizen of yours and has often crossed the sea to be as useful as he could to his native city, always escorting the governors of the province and even accompanying me twice already, the first time escorting me from Ephesos to Rhodes and now on my coming to you from Rhodes. ... Farewell.' (From Ephesus. Translation from Lewis 1974: 26H)

When the newly appointed Prefect of Egypt, Avillius Flaccus, went to his province he apparently travelled across the Adriatic to Greece then over the Aegean to Asia (Philo *In Flaccum* 152). But an entirely overland route across Asia and Syria to Egypt seems unlikely and certainly when he was returned to Rome in disgrace, Flaccus was sent by sea (*In Flaccum* 125): 'He has started on his voyage in early winter and endured a multitude of hardships, tasting of the terrors of the sea also, ... When with difficulty he arrived in Italy....' The advice preserved elsewhere in Philo is instructive:

> When he [the Herodian prince Herod Agrippa I] was about to set out thither [Judaea] Gaius advised him not to undertake the voyage from Brundisium to Syria which was long and wearisome but wait for the etesian winds and take the short route through Alexandria. He told him that thence there were swift-sailing merchant vessels and highly skilled pilots who manage them as a charioteer

7. The structures of the Roman state

manages race-horses and provide a straightforward passage along the direct route.... He went down to Dicaearchia [= Puteoli], and seeing there some ships of Alexandria laying at anchor and ready to sail he embarked with his retinue, and after a good voyage came to land a few days later without being expected or his purposes detected.... [H]e had stayed there [= Alexandria] before on his voyage to Rome to join Tiberius (Philo *In Flaccum* 26-8).

It seems likely that governors of Egypt, exploiting the prevailing winds of the eastern Mediterranean (Casson 1950), would travel by sea direct from southern Italy to Alexandria. We may suppose governors of Judaea would follow the same route and then take the step advocated by Gaius of a swift voyage to their seat of government at Caesarea.

The governors of Arabia were bound to pass through at least one other province to reach their own. By sea to Antioch and on through Syria is a possibility. However, the shortest and swiftest route at least outbound would involve heading for Alexandria then Caesarea as Gaius advises Herod Agrippa (above). And we may recollect the Apostle Paul travelling by sea from Caesarea to Italy on a ship coming from Alexandria (Acts of the Apostles 27.1-28.15). It might depend very much on the season and the perception of safety in a sea voyage.

From Caesarea the route ran to Scythopolis after which one could either travel to Bostra through Gadara or Gerasa. Of all the routes across the Jordan Valley this one had the easiest descent on the west (Roll 2002: 217). In short, an arriving governor might enter on his duties direct, arriving at Bostra via Gadara. As we saw (ch. 4), the road from Caesarea to Scythopolis is dated by a milestone to AD 69, the earliest by far in the wider region. It is believed the extension through Pella to Gerasa (and Philadelphia?) was laid out then or soon after as well (ch. 4.3). In contrast, the slight evidence for the Gadara to

Bostra road belongs to the 160s. In short, arriving governors may well have followed a route through Scythopolis and Pella in Palestine to make the first entry of a city of Arabia at Gerasa. It is possible that Gerasa was also the base for the imperial provincial procurator (below, ch. 7.3). Gerasa would then have organized the formal greeting (and, perhaps, departure) of the retiring governor). Later, when there was a formal road from Gadara to Bostra, governors may have entered their province further north with Adraha or even Bostra itself as the official gateway city. But that would have involved passage through Gadara, too – a city of Palestine. We may conclude this section, therefore, by recollecting the layout of Gadara. The town developed laterally along an east-west ridge. On the west was a succession of monumental gates as the town expanded. Furthest west, just beyond the remains of the incomplete hippodrome, is an immense free-standing arch or gateway. Weber (2000) may well be right to see it as a customs barrier but the monumentality surely implies something different, or more. Regular arrivals/ departures of governors passing through the arch and perhaps then intended to parade through the crowded (but unfinished) hippodrome may have been a common pageant.

7.3. Provincial administration

We know a great deal about Roman provincial administration. The evidence is scattered and fragmentary but, at least for the main lines of administration and its implications, collectively it allows us to construct a cohesive and coherent picture. Applied to Arabia and especially NWJ, we may outline administration as follows.

After AD 106 the key figures in the lives of the inhabitants of Arabia began with the emperor far to the west in central Italy. His name (and image) was on the numerous coins in circulation,

7. The structures of the Roman state

on statuary, on milestones, on dedications erected in cities, on the mass of documents that ordered and controlled their lives (ch. 6). The soldiers of the garrison were paid by him, revered his image set up among their military standards, took an annual oath of loyalty to him and celebrated the great events of his life and reign. For the Nabataean population this was a marked shift from a king based in Petra.

Closer at hand was the representative of the emperor, the governor, one of the most senior members of the small imperial aristocracy. In the case of Arabia, he was also the commander of a legion of some 5000 Roman citizen soldiers, whose senior officers – the six tribunes – were themselves drawn from the same aristocracy: one senator and five from the equestrian order. The governor was assisted by a procurator, a senior member of the equestrian order overseeing financial matters. By the second century AD the equestrian officials and quite often even the senatorial ones were seldom Italian. As we have seen, however, three of the cities of NWJ were attributed to Judaea/ Palaestina and their inhabitants looked not to Bostra but to Caesarea on the Mediterranean coast, and to the governor and procurator of that province.

After 106 the lives of the inhabitants of northern Jordan were re-oriented in varying degrees. For the inhabitants of the Decapolis cities the emperor had long been a major figure in their lives; for the former inhabitants of the Nabataean realm this was a novelty. For all of them, however, the key officials were the governor and procurator. There were many ways in which these men affected the lives of the subject population, but for present purposes I am concerned with impacts which influenced the shape, size and development of the communities that made up the province and especially those of the north.

Imperial government in local centres

Beginning with the formation of Provincia Arabia in AD 106, Bostra became the 'capital' or, as the Romans would have defined it, 'the most frequented city of each province' (6.1). It was the base for the legion assigned to the province with all that that implied in terms of expenditure and cultural and social impact, and it was where the principal imperial officials were normally to be found. Or was it? In fact, both governor and procurator may have been most commonly found elsewhere and in circumstances that would materially affect those places.

First, the evidence for the procurators consists largely of inscriptions honouring them. In the Roman world local communities often set up statues dedicated to the officials who could influence their lives so powerfully. As we have seen (ch. 2), the survival or knowledge of inscriptions is unevenly represented. Nevertheless, it has been noted that while the number of dedications to procurators from the cities of Arabia as a whole is small, the proportion from Gerasa is striking and far greater even than for Bostra. A plausible inference is that the procurator of Arabia was based not at Bostra but at Gerasa (Gatier 1996; cf. Sartre 2003: 613; 2005: 134). The significance for Gerasa of having the principal financial official of the province based at and often resident in the city would be immense. One would have to suppose a residence for him and the staff and friends such aristocratic officials had with them (below). His presence at Gerasa would also define it as a place to which everyone with financial concerns would have to turn. And of course, emperor and procurator corresponded with one another direct, with all that that implies in terms of regular communication between Rome and Gerasa.

More significant, however, and more certain is the impact of the Roman system of justice on specific cities. As is well-known, provincial governors everywhere set off each year on a circuit of

7. The structures of the Roman state

assize centres at which they presided over courts and were available to receive and act on petitions (Burton 1975; Habicht 1975; Marshall 1966; cf. Jones 1978: 65-8). Although this was taking justice to the subject peoples, it was less efficient than it might seem. Everyone intent on a hearing had to present themselves at a local assize centre and simply wait their turn and if necessary follow the governor to his next assize centre if time ran out. One of the newly found papyri from early third-century Mesopotamia relating to such a hearing has the petitioner say he waited for eight months (Feissel and Gascou 1989: 547-9). How long a governor spent in any one place would vary from province to province and even according to the other demands made on him. It would be affected by the number of assize centres and the area any one of them covered.

There were major advantages to being an assize centre. 'Local dignitaries had an unparalleled opportunity to ingratiate themselves with the Roman authorities and to improve their prestige while entertaining the governor in their homes during the assize' (Marshall 1966: 238). The scale of business transacted could be immense. There is the well-known case of a prefect of Egypt in AD 208-10 who, while at Arsinoe, received 1804 petitions over a two-and-a-half-day period (*P.Yale* I: 61; Burton 1975: 102 n. 97; Hopkins 1991: 137 n.9). A Chinese source singles out this feature explicitly among a few characterizing what they knew of Roman administration:

> When the king [= governor] goes out he usually gets one of his suite to follow him with a leather bag, into which petitioners throw a statement of their cases; on arrival at the palace, the king examines into the merits of each case (Hirth 1885: 70-1; Wei-Lo 38).

Moreover, there are strong reasons to believe that central provincial archives were modest (Isaac 1998) and the major caches were held *locally* at the assize centres by the people who had a vested interest in being able to produce documentary evidence in their own hearings (Burton 1975: 103; Ando 2000; 90-6; cf. ch. 6.4).

But it was not just judicial affairs that accrued. Habicht (1975: 90) notes that although the assize centres were created to suit Roman judicial convenience, they could then be used as the basis for other activities involving the communities of a province either for imperial or local business. In Arabia as in Asia they may well have been used as a means of distributing the shares of a collective expense and for other such roles as assisting with census and tax administration, recruitment and selection of members for a provincial council.

Finally, there is the economic role and here we need not simply infer a benefit. This is Dio Chrysostom writing of a small town of Asia in the second century AD whose experience as an assize centre must have been replicated throughout the empire:

> And what is more, the courts are in session every other year in Celaenae, and they bring together an unnumbered throng of people – litigants, jurymen, orators, princes, attendants, slaves, pimps, muleteers, hucksters, harlots, and artisans. Consequently not only can those who have goods to sell obtain the highest prices, but also nothing in the city is out of work, neither the teams nor the houses nor the women. And this contributes not a little to prosperity; for wherever the greatest throng of people comes together, there necessarily we find money in greatest abundance, and it stands to reason that the place should thrive. For example, it is said, I believe, that the district in which the most flocks are quartered proves to be the best for the farmer because of the dung, and indeed many farmers entreat the shepherds to quarter their sheep on their land. So it is, you see, that the business of the courts

7. The structures of the Roman state

is deemed of highest importance toward a city's strength and all men are interested in that as in nothing else. And the foremost cities share this business each in its turn in alternate years (Quaest. 35.15. Trans. Jones 1978).

The documents of the Babatha Archive reveal Petra and Rabbathmoab as assize centres. In November 130 Babatha was summoned to appear before the governor Haterius Nepos at Petra to have him adjudicate on the matter of a date orchard. She is to attend 'every hour and day until judgement' (*P. Yadin* 23) and in July 131 she is called again on the same issue and to attend 'until (she) is heard' (*P. Yadin* 25). As the editor observes, it is clear governors were called upon to adjudicate on what were often very modest affairs with all that implied for the volume of business they transacted.

We don't know the full tally of assize centres in Arabia or Judaea/ Palaestina. In the north there was Bostra. It is certain Gerasa was one: in AD 130 when Hadrian was there an inscription explicitly (according to the restoration) shows him presiding over the assizes – *agora dikon* – throughout his stay in the city (Robert 1934; cf. Jones 1978: 68). The centres were selected for, among other reasons, their locations on a convenient road circuit. Philadelphia was not only an important place but at a nodal point where the old King's Highway and the new *Via Nova Traiana* forked (Fig. 4.2). Of the other cities of northern Jordan, it is possible that one or even both of Gadara and Pella were assize centres for Judaea/ Palaestina; otherwise people from east of the Jordan would have had to travel to, probably, Scythopolis. Further south, the next obvious assize centre was probably Madaba.

It was not just the governor on circuit who would affect such cities and influence their character and development. Again Babatha's documents are instructive. In addition to an assize meeting with the governor at Rabbathmoab in 122 AD, she has to attend there on a prefect of one of the auxiliary regiments of the province to make her census declaration. The census was a regular event in every province and we may confidently suppose a routine procedure by which the population of NWJ made their declarations before the governor or his appointees at, probably, the assize centres where there were established facilities for imperial officials.

The army in Northwest Jordan

Written evidence has always been especially valuable for studying the role and behaviour of the military. First, the cache of papyri of the garrison at Dura Europus on the Middle Euphrates included the remarkable *Feriale Duranum* (*P.Dura* 54) – a calendar of the religious observances required of the soldiers, day by day throughout the year. This example dates to AD 224-35, it is incomplete but highly instructive. The calendar sets out the anniversaries of certain imperial occasions (birthdays, victories, marriages, discharge day) and religious observances (holy days, festivals). It is clear that this was a set of observances which might change through time but was an ordnance applied to the army empire-wide and probably going back two-and-a-half centuries to Augustus in origin.

> What the official policy was is sufficiently apparent from the Feriale Duranum – worship of the gods on whom Rome's welfare depended, loyalty to the emperor and to the memory of good emperors of the past, pride in the earlier achievements of Roman arms, all tempered by traditional merry-making on traditional holidays (Welles et al. 1959: 196).

In short, the calendar gives us a brilliant shaft of illumination into the daily round of the Roman army *everywhere*, including

7. The structures of the Roman state

NWJ, the religious encouragements of the government and the forces at work within the institution that fostered a community through 'corporate' observance (Pollard 2000: 142-3). The probable universality of the calendar, from Syria to Britain, undoubtedly evoked the larger Roman world to which the soldier belonged and which would be visible, too, in varying degrees to civilians within the sound of the army.

Next, as we have seen, the army represented a particularly important island of literacy (ch. 6.4) and the 'epigraphic habit' was deeply embedded. The frequency with which the army inscribed stones recording its building activity is both a testimony to the practice and a vital source of precise information. Military building inscriptions usually have a close date in the wording of the text itself and frequently have a titulature for the emperor which can be dated to a precise year. In conjunction with the evidence of excavation this can be an enormous advantage allowing inferences to be made from the form or style of the structure to other undated places or permitting refinement of such dating material as the vital ceramics. As it happens, NWJ is especially well provided with military building inscriptions (Kennedy 2004b: 25, Fig. 2.1).

7.4. The Roman census

The census is a well-known example of an empire-wide action of the Roman state. Although they were certainly not synchronized across the empire, and direct evidence of a census is entirely lacking for almost every province, we cannot doubt that censuses did take place regularly and that they were significant events for the population. We know, for example, that censuses were regarded with fear and suspicion from the reaction in Judaea in AD 6 (Josephus, *Antiquitates Judaicae* XVII.355-XVIII.1-4; cf. *Bellum Judaicum* II.111; VII.253. Cf. Tacitus *Annals* 6.40). We know most about the census in Egypt and almost all the several hundred examples of census returns we have are for that province. Two recent calculations concerning the Egyptian census are illuminating: Hopkins (1991: 133) (cf. ch. 6.4), assuming a population of 3.5 million and household sizes averaging five people, calculated that each of Egypt's quite well-attested 14-year census cycles would have produced c. 700,000 returns. Even allowing for a low population he calculates we might expect almost 12 million census returns for the period. In fact we have less than 1000. Scheidel (2001a: 142), assuming a population fluctuating between five and six million and an average household of 4.3 arrives at c. 1.3 million returns each time.

Until recently Arabia was like almost every province. There was no evidence of a census either in a literary reference or from the survival of a census return. That has changed with the discovery in the Babatha Archive of a copy of a property census return for AD 127 (*P.Yadin* 16) (ch. 6). There is no reason to doubt it was part of a regular census encompassing the entire province or at least the part recently annexed when the Nabataean kingdom came to an end in AD 106.

Here is a marvellous example of what has been called the 'entanglement' of people in writing (Moreland 2001: 94, 97, 109; cf. above ch. 6). And not just in writing but in several languages. Simultaneously to Babatha's declaration at Rabbathmoab, people throughout the province were doubtless following suit there and at Petra, Gerasa and, presumably, all of the major centres of the province.

We do not know the population size of Arabia or NWJ Jordan at any point but we can use the numbers suggested in ch. 5.4 of c. 500,000. If we adopt a household size of five, the result is that each census in NWJ would involve the completion of c. 100,000 returns and several million in total (assuming a 14-year interval – cf. Isaac 1994: 264 for a 10-year cycle; Duncan-Jones 1994: 59-63 for a possible 15-year cycle). Nor is that the end of the

7. The structures of the Roman state

matter. In Egypt at least, there is good evidence for multiple copies being made for lodging with various officials/ archives. In one case there are six copies. There is also further evidence that individuals might themselves retain a copy, just as Babatha opted to do. The evidence is slight and ambiguous for whether officials also issued receipts as proof of declaration (Bagnall and Frier 1994: 19-21). The organization of all this and of the lists extracted from the declarations is hinted at in an Egyptian papyrus of AD 132/3 where nine scribes are contracted to provide specified derivative documents (*P.Mich.* XI: 603).

Apart from this attested occasion, there will have been censuses at regular intervals in Arabia throughout the second century and parts of the third (and, of course, in those parts formerly belonging to Syria in the preceding century). On each occasion, presumably for at least several weeks, officials had to interact in a novel way with the vast majority of the population in a complex and labour-intensive activity. As most people were insufficiently literate, much of the documentation would have had to be done for them. The formulaic nature of the declaration also required professionals who knew *what* to write. In the major towns that might involve the scribes of the permanent local bureaucracy; in the smaller towns it seems literate military personnel were employed as in Babatha's case; it might even involve teams of travelling scribes (Bagnall and Frier 1994: 17-18). A huge quantity of 'paper' (and ink and pens) would have been required over and above normal consumption with all that that implies in terms of production, transport, expense and distribution. The logistics would be demanding even today – Babatha and her guardian travelled some distance then had to wait till their turn came then longer still while a copy was made for them. For the ancient world this was probably close to the limits of what a pre-industrial society could organize. Even after registration details had been completed documentation had to be archived in, probably, a variety of local

Gerasa and the Decapolis

centres. We may suppose Gerasa was one of those (ch. 7.3). It must be stressed that we have not a single item of direct evidence for any of this in NWJ and only this one property census for Arabia as a whole. But we cannot doubt that these censuses occurred, that they disrupted and probably caused acute anxiety among a largely uneducated and fearful population and likely enough increased the incidence of petty tyrannies and corruption for many in the course of this vast and threatening intrusion by the state into people's lives.

8

Everyday life

It is a truism that the Roman empire was a pre-industrial society. As such, many of the structural features of such societies apply to it and, with caution, we may insist on some of those as basic features of NWJ in the early empire.

8.1. Health, disease and poverty

Everything we know of pre-industrial populations makes it clear that life in the countryside was healthier than in the town. Indeed, cities, all cities, were population sinks, drawing in people from the countryside. Large and concentrated populations made diseases more likely, deadly and inescapable; urban conditions killed their populations faster than they could be replaced. If great care was not taken to protect stored foodstuffs and remove even human waste from the urban areas, rats throve and via their fleas spread a raft of diseases deadly to humans (Engels 1999: 14-17). There is no reason to doubt that this was true of the cities of NWJ. However, we should be careful. These cities were relatively small (5.3-5.4) with consequent limits on the extent to which they could be victims of the routine crowd epidemics of larger centres. Moreover, in Roman times cities took important steps to limit the agents of deadly illness and disease even if they were not necessarily conscious of those consequences. The paving of streets was an important factor is minimizing the effects of contaminating waste in the midst of the community; latrines were available and urine would be collected to use in fulling, while the ubiquitous drains/

sewers carried off much polluted water and human waste; major efforts were made to protect stored foodstuffs from contamination; and something as obvious as the cat – domesticated in the Near East long before – would keep down the dangerous rat population (Engels 1999: ch. 3) Water was brought into the city and if it was not always as clean as might be, the widespread evidence for the large-scale production of wine in the ancient world in general – including NWJ where Capitolias/ Beit Ras in particular was famed for its wine (Lentzen and Knauf 1987: 35-6; cf. Watson 2004) – will have benefited many who could drink it instead of or along with water.

The baths were immensely popular and each of the dozen cities in the region probably had at least one. Two large establishments are known at Gerasa of the second century AD, another at Gadara and two at Bostra. The rich might prefer to bathe at home or could attend public baths before the wider populace was allowed in; an entry fee, though small, could exclude the chronically poor (and dirty). Before the modern use of chemicals and filtering, the water of public baths must have become progressively more contaminated as it was used by people not just for washing themselves but to soothe – on medical advice – wounds, boils and haemorrhoids (Scheidel 2003: 160). But then these same places that echoed daily to the cries of people bathing or hawking food or trinkets may also – as we now know was the case with the Baths of Hadrian at Antioch in AD 245 (Feissel and Gascou 1989: 545-57) – have served as convenient locations for the governor's assize courts (ch. 7.3). What were places of recreation and entertainment may also have been places of terrifying justice (Shaw 2003).

Conversely, much of the rural population lived in villages rather than isolated farmsteads. Some of these were quite large. Umm el-Jimal, for example, even on a low estimate, is thought to have had a population of *c.* 2500-3000 (De Vries 1998: 111); perhaps half or a third of the population of Gerasa.

8. Everyday life

It did not have paved streets, there were no drains/ sewers, human waste collected in the latrines identified in many houses must have been an immediate health hazard and it may later have been spread on the adjacent fields. Perhaps worse still, many of the houses, two or three storeys high, involved humans living upstairs above stables and barns. The common deadly diseases which are believed to have migrated from domestic animals to humans had already long before made this shift. However, living with your stock still has its disadvantages: 'many peasant farmers live and sleep close to cows and their feces, urine, breath, sores, and blood'. Summing up:

> ... farmers are sedentary and live amid their own sewage, thus providing microbes with a short path from one person's body into another's drinking water. ... Some farming populations make it even easier for their own fecal bacteria and worms to infect new victims, by gathering their feces and urine and spreading them as fertilizer on the fields where people work. ... Sedentary farmers become surrounded not only by their feces but also by disease-transmitting rodents, attracted by the farmers' stored food (Diamond 1997: 205-7).

Poverty

Literary sources allude to beggars and poverty in towns. In the pagan period such social welfare as one encounters – such as the provision of food on occasions or financial support for orphans – are rare outside Italy and overwhelmingly aimed at fellow citizens of the community – the 'deserving poor' – rather than the needy as such (Whittaker 1993; cf. Shaw 2002). Even after the spread of Christianity, concern for the poor was strictly limited even if they were much more visible because the church institutionalized concern for them (Brown 2001).

In all periods, as Whittaker noted (1993: 275), 'mass poverty in both ancient and modern preindustrial societies was (and still is) overwhelmingly a rural phenomenon hence it is rarely documented'. Towns provided for themselves or were assisted by imperial intervention in times of shortage. Crop failures and famine were common – every four or five years in Europe in the period before the eighteenth century (Whittaker 1993: 281). The highlands of NWJ offer good soils and abundant rainfall but the villages of the pre-desert at least were operating in marginal lands and low rainfall and would have had precarious existences for which towns could make no provision – indeed, they were likely to expel those of their own inhabitants who were slaves or foreigners. We may note, too, the recent argument that the evidence for a large population in late Roman times should be viewed as a sign not of success but of dangerous overpopulation (Frier 2001).

8.2. Seasonality of birth, marriage and death in the Decapolis

Modern cities have long since broken away from the grosser calendrical imperatives of their farming hinterlands. In the ancient world, however, as for all pre-industrial societies, there was a powerful link between the economic imperatives of the farmer and the calendar of the urban dweller (Shaw 1997: 75), which are reflected in the patterns to the great rituals of life.

Birth

Studies of modern societies reveal some striking similarities and differences. For example, there is a very similar birthing pattern extending across northwestern Europe, Canada and the northern part of the USA; that pattern is almost exactly reversed in the rest of the USA. Although much more limited and often uneven, there is enough evidence to demonstrate the

8. Everyday life

seasonality of birthing for the ancient world as well. Shaw (2001a: 102) concludes that with the striking exception of Egypt – where the pattern is almost the reverse, the birthing pattern around the Mediterranean in early modern and, as far as we can tell, Roman times, too, was for 'a long-wave cycle of much higher numbers of births in the late autumn and winter months and much lower rates in the intervening periods. This pattern of birthing suggests more intensive cycles of procreative activity in the months between April and June of each year.' Not just 'more intensive cycles ... of procreative activity' but perhaps an improved fertility – these are the months when diet might be improving after the long winter and conception become more likely.

Death

The seasonality of death in the city of Rome itself is attributable to the incidence of malaria during the summer months (Sallares 2002: 61, 63, 82; cf. Shaw 1996; Scheidel 2001b: 25-7). Seasonality in death for Roman Egypt is clear but problematic in its application outside the province (Scheidel 2001a: 1-51). Closer to our region, there is the study by Patlagean (1977: 92-4; Scheidel 2001a: 36-7) on the basis of 170 inscriptions from Moab and the late Roman province of Palaestina III of (probably) the fourth to seventh centuries AD. They record the month of death and show a bunching in the period March-July, representing about 60% of all deaths in these five months. Little should be built on this modest collection of epitaphs beyond the probability it suggests seasonality in our region.

Marriage

This is a life-ritual which *may* be chosen by a society in the way that birth cannot reliably and death not at all. The only specific evidence for the seasonality of marriage in the Near East comes from Judaea. It is limited but suggestive. There was a prohibition on marriage during the seven weeks between Passover and Pentecost. This is the period of heaviest labour on the land. More generally, although there might be a religious overlay, in early modern European societies the fundamental guiding factor in seasonality was economic. Agrarian societies tend to avoid those times of the year when 'ploughing, planting and harvesting were dictated by climatic conditions' (Shaw 1997: 59). Around much of the Mediterranean, precise dates of harvest fluctuate but the total package of seasonal work tended to be equally extensive (harvesting of grain, grapes and olives; ploughing and sowing; shearing sheep). The outcome was that marriages took place largely in the 'downtime' which began towards the end of November, peaked in December and January and began to drop in February.

Discussion

In every community, but especially in urban concentrations, people would be confronted in predictable and annual patterns with major familial events according to the effects of the seasons directly on people (death and perhaps birth) or the requirements of the farming calendar (marriage). In practice what that would mean is, broadly:

January-February: marriages relatively common.
March onwards but especially in July to October: deaths relatively common.
September-December: births relatively common and marriages begin to become common from early November.

8.3. Occupations

The Roman empire was one of the most complex societies of the pre-industrial age, and occupational specialization is one way of gauging the extent of that complexity.

8. Everyday life

A scatter of inscriptions from NWJ – most notably Gerasa – provide references to specific occupations: potters, retail traders, goldsmiths, linen workers, etc. The number is disappointingly small and no better even at the provincial capital, Bostra: leaving aside soldiers, imperial officials and a handful of civic functionaries, the tally of occupations is slender and even the presence of slaves is rare. As Sartre (1985: 153-4) says, entire categories we might expect are missing: 'Le monde des boutiquiers et des artisans, plus encore celui des paysans et des proprietaires fanciers nous échappent complètement.' Again we can turn with a high degree of confidence to evidence from other places and times and to simple probability. There is, for instance, the famous example of the several hundred epitaphs of the modest town of Korykos in Cilicia. A combination of the chance of survival and the local fashion for including the occupation of the deceased has revealed information rarely met elsewhere outside Rome itself. Of the 702 texts, over half (366) give the information and these run to a total of 110 distinct named occupations. As Hopkins noted (1978: 72), this contrasts with 85 occupations reported on texts at Pompeii and over 200 at Rome itself. At Korykos, as one might expect, 18% of the named occupations are in textile-making of some kind and 10% in pottery-making. We can hardly doubt that at Gerasa and the neighbouring cities of NWJ, the population also included a hundred or more occupational specializations and that clothing and pottery were especially notable. Indeed, at Gerasa, the linen workers, alone among occupational groups, were allocated an entire section of seating in the odeon (Retzleff and Mjely 2004: 40-1). Nor can we doubt that the towns included prostitutes. Public baths and inns were notorious as the locale of prostitutes (Dauphin 1996) and there is abundant anecdotal evidence from all around the ancient world at every period to make it certain that alongside the monumentality and grandeur of the two great public early Roman baths at Gerasa and

Gerasa and the Decapolis

the splendour of their art works, we need to set the certainty of prostitution (below).

Of course, even without any text from NWJ or anywhere else in the Roman world we could have inferred from the physical remains of the towns, the existence of a wide variety of occupations from day labourers engaged in the back-breaking work of any community through tanners (tanning pits), stone workers (workshops and structures of all kinds), mosaicists (scores of mosaics), bath attendants (public baths), suppliers of fuel (baths and private houses), etc.

Village occupations

We might make the same inferences for the smaller settlements of the region but can also turn to the very illuminating inscriptions from Castellum Celtianum in Africa (Pflaum 1955: 134f.) which record a selection of the people who made up the local commercial life in a small market town: six ploughmen, four tenant farmers, eight harvesters, two donkey-drovers, one each of a goat-herd, a beet-seller, an oyster-woman, cook, innkeeper, strawseller, baker, linen merchant, messenger, shopkeeper, bean-seller, and two *nundinariae* [market-women = prostitutes?]. Even in a small settlement the presence of the last of these should cause no surprise, as anecdotes in late Roman hagiography reveal (Moschos 1992): for example, the hermit who went off to the local village to work off his sexual urges; the Life of St Theodore (3) describes his mother, her sister and his grandmother combining the running of a rural inn with opportunistic prostitution (trans. Dawes and Baynes 1977 [1948]: 88). Closer to NWJ, rabbinic and Roman sources make clear the equation between inns and brothels – which would be hard to identify from the archaeological remains – and the popularity of the market place for prostitution (Sperber 1998: 15-17; Dauphin 1996), while actresses doubled as prostitutes (cf. the apparent

8. Everyday life

explicit reference for AD 250s to a concert party member in a graffito at Dura Europos as a prostitute: *Dura Preliminary Report* 9.1: 203-65).

8.4. Markets

A thin scatter of anecdotes from around the empire refer to local annual fairs and the huge numbers of people attracted from a wide area including, in the case of Batnae in Mesopotamia in AD 354, from beyond the frontier (de Ligt 1993: 74, 89; Ammianus Marcellinus 24.3.3) (cf. ch. 7.3 for markets associated with assizes).

> The town of Batne, founded in Anthemusia in early times by a band of Macedonians, is separated by a short space from the river Euphrates; it is filled with wealthy traders when, at the yearly festival, near the beginning of the month of September, a great crowd of every condition gathers for the fair, to traffic in the wares sent from India and China, and in other articles that are regularly brought there in great abundance by land and sea.

Other anecdotes report local frequent market activity, what are known as periodic markets (*nundinae*) and commonly associated with villages. In North Africa a series of Latin inscriptions provides fascinating references to periodic markets in villages or places designated on great estates and to their regularity throughout the year (Shaw 1979; 1981 [= 1995a: I with additional notes at pp. 10-13]). Chance has preserved this concentration of evidence there because the region had been extensively colonized generations before by Italian migrants and a number of them embraced 'the epigraphic habit' and incised the important details of markets and the authority for them on stone. Not a single such inscription or literary reference survives for Arabia, much less NWJ. The best we have is some literary evidence for what may be periodic markets in the villages around Antioch in Syria (Libanius *Oratio* II.230) and, of course, the annual fairs at not just Batnae in Mesopotamia but at Baetocaece in Syria and near Hebron in Palestine (de Ligt 1993). However, as the scholar who has done so much to illuminate these *nundinae* in Africa repeatedly stresses, local periodic markets were natural, vital and certainly existed in their thousands throughout the Roman empire (Shaw 1981: 46-7). In short, even without the explicit evidence for any *nundinae* in NWJ we can infer their existence and direct that knowledge to helping interpret and explain the settlement pattern of the region.

As for what was on sale and how it was measured, we may turn from the silence of NWJ to the words of the Palmyra Tax Law (Matthews 1984: esp. 174-80). Goods are measured in camel- or donkey-loads; they may be carried in goatskins and alabaster vessels; produce includes salt, purple-dyed fleece, animal fat, salt fish, olive oil, unguent, bronze statues, animals for slaughter and camel skins; and there are taxes on slaves and a sliding scale on prostitutes. There is every reason to assume the situation would be very similar in NWJ in Gadara or Gerasa.

8.5. Miscellaneous

Sacrifices and offerings

Animal sacrifices are not mentioned in relation to the temples of NWJ. Nevertheless, it would have been a feature of *all* cities that animals were routinely sacrificed. We are told this indirectly by the Younger Pliny in a letter from Bithynia when he reports (*Epistulae* 10.96.10) that after his action against local Christians, the demand for sacrificial animals revived. The dedication of millions of mummified animals was unique to Egypt, yet the very fact of the enterprise, known almost entirely

8. Everyday life

because the animal was being preserved rather than burnt, should alert us to the scale on which such activities *could* exist. We can hardly doubt the significance of an 'industry' in sacrificial animals in the Decapolis, not least in the huge temples of Zeus and Artemis at Gerasa. A corollary to this may be seen in the protest of the Ephesian silversmiths that their trade in religious souvenirs was undermined by Christians (Acts of the Apostles 19.23.7). There were probably souvenirs available at all major temples and that might well apply to those of the Decapolis – indeed, it may explain the terracotta models of deities and rider figures recovered in the so-called 'Potter's Workshop' at Gerasa (Iliffe 1945).

A chance reference in the fifth century AD historian Zosimus (I.58) tells is something we might have guessed:

> At Aphaca, between Heliopolis and Byblos, there is a temple to Aphrodite Aphacitis, near which is a pond like an artificial tank. ... The people gathered there used to throw into the pond in honour of the goddess gifts of gold and silver or clothing of linen, silk or other precious material, and if they were accepted the light and heavy things both sank, but if rejected both the cloth and anything of gold, silver or other material which naturally sinks could be seen floating on the water.

Zosimus goes on to explain that offerings made by a Palmyrene delegation at the festival in 271 floated to the surface at the festival in 272, the year Aurelian captured and sacked the city. Apart from listing the kinds of offerings that might be made, the implication is that cities routinely sent delegations to make dedications to religious festivals in honour of major deities at even quite distant places. In fact, though without much detail, Herodian (V.3.4) had already in the early third century reported princelings all around Emesa sending offerings to its great temple of Elagabalus. We may reasonably suppose that applied to the major cult centres of the Decapolis, not least the two great temples to Artemis and Zeus at Gerasa.

Names and meanings

Names are common in texts – of people, peoples and places. Tombstones and local dedications give us the names of numerous individuals, mainly males and certainly just those wealthy enough to afford an epitaph. The names can be instructive – Semitic, Greek and some that are Roman (actually Italian) in origin or romanized versions of local names. It is often less tidy than we would like. A man with Greek or Roman names whose patronymic is Semitic implies a stage in the hellenization/ romanization of a family: 'Diodoros son of Zebsaos [Zebedas?]' (Seigne 1985: 289-91). That dates to AD 27/8, but just a few years earlier in AD 22/3 we have 'Zabdion son of Aristomachos' (Welles at Kraeling 1938: 373-4, no. 2), a man with a Greek name giving at least one child a Semitic one.

Even the name of the city is problematic and suggestive. Although officially Antioch on the Golden River, it was evidently popularly known as Gerasa, derived from the semitic name (Gersu?) for the pre-Greek settlement. Three inscriptions from Gerasa actually spell out this confusion in identity, all of them (significantly) from the reign of Hadrian: e.g. *Antioch[i]/ae ad Chrysorhoan quae/ et Gerasa* (Antioch on the Chrysorhoas known as Gerasa) (Welles at Kraeling 1938: 390-1, no. 30). The evidence of Gerasa and the ease with which Semitic names re-appeared after AD 637, underscores the lingering and perhaps always significant Semitic character of these Graeco-Roman cities. Philadelphia, formerly Rabbath Ammon and after the Islamic conquest again Amman, seems to have maintained officially at least its Greek identity for a

8. Everyday life

thousand years and is never identified in any other form. But we have few inscriptions for Philadelphia (ch. 2.1). However, we have an instructive epitaph found at Carnuntum in Pannonia (Austria) (*ILS* 9168), probably dating to AD 69:

Proculus Rabili f(ili) Col(lina tribu), Philadel(phia), mil(es) optio coh(ortis) II Italic(ae) c(ivium) R(omanorum) (centuria) Fa[us]tino, ex vexil(latione) sagit(tariorum) exer(citus) Syriaci stip(endia) VII, vixit an(norum) XXVI. Apuleius frater f(aciendum) c(uravit).

(Proculus, the son of Rabilus, of the Tribe Collina, of Philadelphia, Soldier and Optio of the Cohort II Italica Civium Romanorum, Century of Faustinus, of the detachment of archers from the Syrian army. Served for 7 years, lived 26. Apuleius his brother undertook the making of this.)

Proculus and Apuleius have Roman names and citizenship but the latinised form of their father's name cannot hide its Semitic origin, as Nabataean Rabel.

Beneath the 'Pella' and 'Antioch' and 'Philadelphia', these places were probably still thought of, even by many of their own citizens, as semitic. In that respect, Gadara was more open about its identity with an unchanged semitic name.

Other

Finally, a few other features of society we would be hard put to identify without written evidence. Babatha's Archive is a mine of explicit and useful information about contemporary society and culture (Lewis 1989; ch. V). For example, it shows small landowners with property in two widely separated areas – not unexpected but impossible to identify archaeologically. They also show her second husband, apparently quite openly, practising polygamy or bigamy. The consensus had been that this was rare by this time except perhaps among the elite. Related to this is the status and position of women and children in society. The layout of houses and depiction of women in art might allow inferences, but a single text revealing that even an heiress needed to be represented in public affairs by a male, speaks directly to us (*P.Yadin* 16). Likewise the new Petra papyri explicitly reveal people at Petra owning land – and in dispute over it – in Zodocatha, 25 km southeast of Petra (Koenen and Kaimio 1997).

The limitations of written evidence are, of course, numerous and too well known to need a detailed exposition. The uneven patterns in inscribing and survival or discovery are the most obvious. The meaning of texts, too, is highly problematic. And, of course, dating is often not clear – dating by consular year or provincial era or imperial titulature is precise but rare and the largest group of our texts, tombstones, is often simply a mass of material only broadly attributable to a span of two or three centuries. But even the bigger questions are exasperatingly elusive. For example, the fact of a great empire-wide plague in the Antonine period is known and agreed. What is not agreed is how serious it was and even how one may hope to demonstrate it. NWJ would surely have been as affected but we cannot identify, quantify or see consequences (cf. De Vries 1998: 240). On the other hand, it is the existence of varied categories of evidence that enriches study of the period. The evidence of destruction at Dura Europos and now at Zeugma might well be interpreted by archaeologists as closely contemporary and part of a major war. The written sources not only allow greater precision in dating but reveal a catalogue of other major places destroyed at the same time, the agents of the destruction, the context and the fact that it was part of a much greater upheaval.

9

Where to next?

... changes are the stuff of history

MacMullen 1990: 8

A. CHANGE

9.1. Overview

The 'virtual island' of Northwest Jordan underwent significant, indeed, unique changes during the Long Classical Millennium. Modest 'urban centres' of the Late Iron Age became true cities by the early Roman period. Their character, though always essentially indigenous, acquired many of the key elements of Classical civilization, from the civic magistracies of a Greek polis to the extensive use of the Greek language. They are marked by impressive architectural furniture from the functional (purpose-built market halls: *macella*), through the aesthetic (colonnaded streets), the recreational (theatres), to the religious (great temples and, later, churches). The overall impression is of prosperity, but the rises and falls that must have occurred during these centuries are largely invisible to us. Instead, we must work largely with the crude fact that they seem to have developed slowly during the Hellenistic period then burst forth under Roman rule and been sustained at a high level through to the early Islamic period.

During this same period we see an increasingly thick settlement of the countryside. Not just farmsteads and villages in the arable, well-watered highlands but their dramatic extension into the pre-desert where forts and roads provided security and opened up 'frontier' lands. But these were not empty places – nomads had long strewn the desert beyond with thousands of distinctive structures and the pre-desert was part of their world. At broadly the same time as cities were acquiring their most significant public architecture, these same nomads wrote tens of thousands of brief messages across a wide swathe of the Basalt Desert. About the time regarded as that of the transition from pagan Classical Antiquity to Christian Late Antiquity – the third and fourth centuries AD, the nomadic writing ceased but in the pre-desert and even the Basalt Desert in places, modest settlements developed into villages and small towns.

A characteristic feature of many of these new settlements in the pre-desert is the abundance of churches, far more than one would expect in such modest places. Some of these churches were still functioning into the Islamic period; the villages themselves throve well into the eighth century, a distinctive feature of the region. Also characteristic of this early Islamic period are the luxury mansions that sprang up in the pre-desert and desert, the residences of grandees of the new ruling class or perhaps members of the Umayyad family itself.

There are traces throughout the region of the ingenuity of humankind in exploiting its opportunities and confronting its challenges. Fossilised terraces abound throughout the highland zone; long tunnels brought water into the cities (Häser 2004); water powered a stone saw at Gerasa (Seigne 2002) and some of the mediaeval grain mills along the neighbouring water courses may have an earlier origin; thousands of rock-cut cisterns stored water for domestic use and great reservoirs provided for flocks; simple cross walls on wadis in the pre-desert allowed limited farming and old field boundaries can still be traced here and there; and some of the ancient tracks of the region were progressively developed into all-weather Roman roads which transformed communications. Roads are marked

9. Where to next?

in many cases by milestones, usually inscribed. This other technology – writing – becomes ubiquitous in this period, probably tens of millions of items being produced, though mainly on perishable materials.

Finally, the range and quantity of artefacts increased significantly. Sites of all kinds are strewn with a wide variety of pottery types, excavations reveal mosaics and wall-paintings and unlooted tombs produce lamps, ceramic and glass vessels, metalwork, and hint at lost organic items. Artefacts are often locally made but there is a steep increase in the numbers imported from further afield. And, of course, coins become far more abundant in numbers and types, both Roman imperial and locally minted. The coins hint at the presence of the soldiers – paid regularly in coin, whose forts are so prominent in the pre-desert and desert, and at the commerce that passed along the trade routes from Arabia and the Gulf.

The world of early Islamic NWJ would have included much that was familiar to the people of 500 years – even 1000 years – earlier. And a great deal that would have astonished them. Some were developments, predictable outcomes of patterns, visible in the Late Iron Age and Hellenistic period. Foremost would be the steady development of cities in size and elaboration and the spread of settlement. Not predictable was the form that development took and the unparalleled extent and scale of settlement. Then there would be the changed political order from 'Greek' kings in Alexandria or Antioch to equally pagan Roman emperors in Rome or Christian ones in Constantinople, to Muslim Arab caliphs in nearby Damascus. This astonishing development might have masked the near-elimination of the other and older monotheistic religion of this remarkable corner of the world, Judaism. The numerous churches and now mosques would contrast with the ruined or re-used pagan temples. A region that had largely looked west was now firmly part of an 'East' stretching from Morocco to Central Asia. And

Gerasa and the Decapolis

the pious rulers and increasingly its wider population looked to the holy places of central Arabia and were closely bound to the nomads of the wider region. Not predictable either would have been the duration of this period with a real continuity extending over some 1200 years. And surprising, had they been able to look ahead, would have been the quite rapid decline in settlement, never again to be reached before the mid-twentieth century.

9.2. Explaining change

The dynamics of change are, as yet, impossible to define with any confidence. At opposite extremes one may point to the Pax Romana and a more favourable climate. Both may well have been powerful forces for change singly or in happy coincidence. The centuries-long duration of widespread peace, stability and stable government should not be underestimated. But these mainly provided vital, but *passive*, conditions for development rather than *actively* encompassing it; and they would promote largely predictable development rather than change. Nor would it necessarily explain the unparalleled extent and scale of settlement. After all, as one recent commentator has stressed (Johns 1994: 7; cf. ch. 2.3 above), what needs to be explained in the wide sweep of Near Eastern history is not why an arid region has limited scope for development but why in one period alone it seemed to break through the limit of the possible. Climate change is a factor newly returned to vogue as a serious contender (ch. 3.6); it needs now to be shown to co-relate with the archaeological evidence and its character and possible impact need to be defined more closely.

Other explanations are legion. The significant factor may not have been 'peace' alone but the nature of the Roman empire itself. Not just another empire in a long sequence to dominate the region from Hittites, Assyrians and Babylonians to Ottomans and the British. Rather, an empire, a civilization which

9. Where to next?

is almost 'modern' in some respects and almost broke through the Malthusian ceiling on population growth. An empire whose remarkable inclusiveness marked it out in history and gave it great cohesion and vitality. It was an empire, too, of the written word on a scale unparalleled till a millennium later, with all that implies about organization and transmission of knowledge (to take but two aspects).

Economic factors must also be explored. NWJ has only a limited area suited to arable farming and capable of producing surpluses. The integration of the region into the wider economic unit of the Near East and Mediterranean world beyond permitted a significant change: farmers could now engage in crop specialization suited to their local conditions and trade their increased surpluses for what they needed. Specialization in food production would be paralleled by occupational specialization in 'manufacture' and the commerce in foodstuffs paralleled by trade in other items. Overlying both of these were the effects of long-distance trade between Arabia, the Gulf and beyond (cf. Young 2001: ch. 3). This cannot yet be quantified in any useful way beyond the impression conveyed by artefact finds and a consensus that there was a quickening of activity as conditions eased the process, and the immense market of the Roman empire, and its urban consumers in particular, demanded luxuries.

Social factors were surely at work, too. The dense network of cities in NWJ created a substantial urban population which would have felt more remote from their rural hinterland and more integrated with one another. Despite the sometimes heavy and increasingly controlling hand of Rome, urban elites at least in the early Roman period managed their own affairs on a significant level. They were literate and even if Greek was not their only or even first language, it became the lingua franca that bound them together, to urban elites elsewhere and to the Roman empire. The region produced a striking number of men of letters (Schürer 1979: II, 49). Although it is unquantifiable, the immense visible and inferable increase in writing suggests a significant increase in literacy. The scale undoubtedly fell far short of what would have been required to create the kind of civil society of much more recent times, yet it was not negligible and may have been an influential component in change.

Political economists might point to the possibility for key social groups to take advantage of conditions (peace and security, political stability and improved government, improved communications) to exploit opportunities (supplying the military, taking advantage of military supply routes, providing services to garrisons, farming and occupational specialization, trade over short and long distances) in their own self-interest which collectively benefited the community. Certainly that might be the case as far as the fuller exploitation of land-holdings or the expansion into new lands was the case. But there is no significant manufacturing. Then, too, we might explore the theory of Hopkins that the imposition of taxation and regular rents actually stimulated production to create surpluses to pay these (Hopkins 1980; cf. 2002). Speculation might lead us, too, into seeing the 'success' of the period and place in terms of the fortuitous interaction or even tension between parts creating unexpected and productive conditions.

The LCM, especially the 'Roman' centuries, saw the emergence of a large population. That might simply be a matter of the conditions defined above. But there are other possibilities. In more recent times in England, the growth of prosperity saw a shift downwards in age at marriage recorded in parish records which in turn lengthened the female fertility period and underwrote a large part of the rapid population rise in what is called the Long Eighteenth Century (Wrigley 1983; 1998). Did something similar occur in the Roman Near East? Did growing prosperity stimulate population increase which in turn became the dynamo for settlement growth?

9. Where to next?

B. DATA AND ANALYSIS

The preceding chapters have explored evidence and methodologies, landscapes and a variety of themes. None has been treated comprehensively and the list of themes could have been extended considerably. The preceding section has explored the nature of change. It remains now to set out a few suggestions for what may be done to enable us to answer such questions more fully. Some will remain elusive; others are capable of clarification.

9.3. Survey

NWJ during the Long Classical Millennium is a region of great riches. But much of the data is the result of the vagaries of survival, of a focus by archaeologists on specific sites or parts of sites, or was acquired opportunistically in the face of development. Early ground surveys encompassed large areas but were superficial; later ones have been intensive and their publication will provide far more comprehensive and reliable data that has ever been available before. It will not be problem-free as recent debates have stressed – ground surveys, no matter how sophisticated, are problematic (Alcock and Cherry 2004). But they remain the best way forward for exploring, interpreting and explaining wide ancient landscapes.

In the case of NWJ we may combine ground survey with the interpretation of old photographs and active aerial reconnaissance (Dyson 2003: ch. 3). The latter have been astonishingly successful in demonstrating graphically how densely used the ancient landscape was – not just the arable highlands and plains but the pre-desert and even desert. Early extensive surveys such as that by Glueck (1934-51) gave no serious hint of either the scale or the extent now being revealed. For the desert in particular, ground survey alone is not a serious option – the area is too large and the remains are often too embedded in the landscape and difficult to see much less interpret. Aerial survey can resolve much of that problem but then is often not able to tell us about date or chronology. Nevertheless, a programme of aerial reconnaissance has the potential to combine highly effectively with ground survey. As the intensive interpretation of the old photographs around Umm el-Jimal demonstrated (Kennedy 1998a; cf. ch. 4.4 above), a great deal can be done to 'people' a landscape.

Two paths are obvious. First, the urgent publication of recent intensive ground surveys and the implementation of a major survey in the key area of the Jarash Basin itself (Kennedy 2004a). Second, the intensive interpretation of the air photographs of the Southern Hauran area (Kennedy 1997; cf. 1998a) has to be extended across the entire region and complemented by systematic ground verification of key sites or site types and by integrating the evidence with that from new dedicated flying. Three of the simplest but most useful projects would be mapping the roads and tracks of the region; mapping the distribution and pattern of kites, wheel-houses and all the other traces of man in the Basalt Desert; and defining the extent of evidence for arid land farming.

A key feature of an intensive ground survey should be an environmental study. That remains a desideratum for NWJ. The recent work by Israeli archaeologists and the startling proposal of a significant climatic change during the LCM underscores the potential and significance and even sheds some light on Jordan, too. Likewise the beginning made by Lucke and his colleagues is important but still falls far short of what is required. Rainfall patterns are vital to understanding the farming base of the region yet we have only modern data to work with. We can look forward to further work on tree rings but potentially much more useful would be the sort of environmental data that should be locked in the deposits of the Azraq Oasis but has been so little explored (Garrard et al. 1985;

9. Where to next?

Gilbertson et al. 1985). On a more detailed level, the extraction of environmental data should be a central part of every excavation and ground survey in the region. How that may be achieved can be seen by turning to the work done recently in the Wadi Faynan in southern Jordan (e.g. Barker 2000) by some of the same people previously engaged in the magisterial UNESCO Libyan Valleys Survey (Barker et al. 1996).

The existing data for the region is immense and the publication of current projects will swell that still further. The development of Geographic Information System software and its adaptation for archaeological projects has provided a powerful tool for storing, manipulating and interpreting this data. A desideratum now is to establish a GIS database to handle the considerable range and quantity of information and that which will be generated in the future.

9.4. Places

The emphasis on survey should not distract from the need to have a better understanding of specific places in a way that can only be achieved by excavation. It seems likely that excavation will continue at Gerasa, Pella, Gadara and perhaps Abila, and probably at Bostra and Scythopolis. The recent discovery of a large theatre at Beit Ras/ Capitolias may stimulate excavation there, too. Fieldwork has halted at Esbus but publication continues and there is now the tremendously important excavation underway at Madaba (Harrison et al. 2003; Foran et al. 2004). But there are astonishing gaps. We know almost nothing about private housing in any of these cities and it might well require an extensive programme and deliberate shifting of emphasis from public buildings to provide enough useful data. Equally serious is that some cities are almost unknown. Not just the small ones such as Livias, Abila and Besimoth in the Peraea but the seemingly large and important city of Gadora (modern

Salt). Even Philadelphia (Amman) is poorly understood despite its size and importance. Even worse is how little can be said about Beit Ras (Capitolias), the Classical town beneath Irbid (Arbela?), and the most striking of all, Dera'a (Adraha).

It is encouraging that there has been a shift to exploring the towns of the region such as Umm el-Jimal, Khirbet es-Samra and Umm er-Resas, and several villages. But a far larger number needs to be explored systematically and there are some key places in this respect. Most notable is Rihab. The 15 churches there and the military inscriptions are suggestive – perhaps a meeting point of and with nomads. But the extent and character of the town is almost unknown; and it is disappearing swiftly as the modern settlement sprawls across more land every year. A systematic survey of the town and its vicinity would be invaluable. Likewise, the well-preserved ruins of the small town of Umm es-Surab just northwest of Jimal offer an opportunity to explore another town and to encompass both Surab and Jimal in a systematic intensive survey of their vicinity in conjunction with air photo interpretation. Possibly playing a comparable role further south is Umm er-Resas where again there is no hinterland survey (ch. 4.4). As for smaller places, villages and farmsteads are numerous but we know little about the former and almost nothing about the latter. Within the context of a survey of the Surab-Jimal hinterland, excavation of the two different types of 'farm' just south of Jimal could teach us a great deal (Fig. 4.6). Finally, excavations at Qasr el-Hallabat need published fully and this key place set in its local context of settlement, roads, routes and nomadic works.

In the immediate future, a great deal can be achieved in terms of understanding settlement by simply gathering the evidence for the hundreds of villages and even more numerous farms in the region and setting out such data as there is as a context for the cities – which all too often seem like islands in an empty landscape.

9. Where to next?

A key to interpretation is chronology, of course. The intensive and long-established excavations at the major cities of the region have done much to establish a ceramic chronology, which can be applied to surface collections at every other site. But more needs to be done to transform the simple breakdown set out in ch. 4 above into something more sophisticated. We are a long way from the degree of nuanced interpretation and explanation Alcock provided for Roman Greece (1993).

C. INTERPRETATIONS

9.5. Nomads and traders

Nomads almost certainly represent a small part of the overall population of the region in any period. However, they are a part that can be highly disruptive of settled farming, as nineteenth-century accounts from Ottoman Syria demonstrate so graphically (Jabbur 1995: App. 2). They can act, too, as a barometer for change in the crucial marginal areas as some shift from nomadism to semi-nomadism or even become sedentarized.

There has been a growing interest in nomads around the world in recent years, and the sophisticated interpretations offered by Whittow and Johns (ch. 2) are exciting pointers to the potential of exploring this aspect of the region still further. In particular we may give much more thought to the sensible observation of Johns that what is of interest in the settlement of the pre-desert is why the nomads apparently were significantly more sedentarized in the 'Roman' period than in any other before or since. We may also learn much from Whittow's suggestions for *how* a nomadic group could become as powerful as those we encounter in the late Roman period (ch. 2.3).

The land in which nomads lived was one through which trade routes passed, and this is a neglected area of research. We have swung in recent years from Rostovtzeff's view (1932) of a city like Jarash as a 'caravan city' to the more recent view that only

Palmyra was truly one (Millar 1998). Even if the cities of the Decapolis were only marginally dependent on caravan trade for their economic well-being the existence of trade routes – not least the great routes up the Wadi Sirhan to Azraq and that which made use of the King's Highway/ *Via Nova Traiana* or the possible '*Via Militaris*' to its east – must have been of importance. First, for the nomads who could support or obstruct them. Second, for the cities. Even if only a small proportion of their income, that could be the difference that underwrote their evident prosperity.

9.6. Arid-land farming

The recent collection of essays on this theme (Barker and Gilbertson 2000) has gone a long way to revealing the wide range of ways in which pre-desert landscapes of the kind we encounter in NWJ can be exploited and what the imperatives are. Especially interesting is the suggestion that people simply adjusted seasonally to a boom-bust economy. However, only one essay (Newson 2000) explicitly looks at part of this region and there is far more scope for interpreting the patterns preserved there. Once again, however, the way ahead will follow from the fuller mapping of what is visible on air photographs and recorded in ground surveys.

The period is a long one and, though a broad outline of development is possible (ch. 4), the unseen nuances and fluctuations can be vital. All too often dating is broad and may be exaggerating later periods at the expense of those in which growth and development began.

*

The Near East is the neglected part of the ancient world. Compared to northwest Europe, the region has attracted little

9. Where to next?

attention, limited resources and relatively few scholars. Despite the recent publication of four books on Roman Syria/ the Near East, it remains grossly understudied (ch. 1.2). However, broad surveys like these will play their role in stimulating further research. An encouraging sign is the very different approaches adopted by these authors (Kennedy 2006a: 365). For too long there were often so few scholars engaged in research on the region that there was little or no debate as individuals had no colleagues to challenge them. The role of the Roman army has emerged as an exception, and interpretation of the meaning of 'Safaitic' inscriptions and of the 'Arab' identity of nomads are others. Nascent research on climate and environment, on villages, religion and farming are all encouraging signs. There is scope for far more.

Bibliography

Alcock, S. (1993) *Graecia Capta. The Landscapes of Roman Greece,* Cambridge
Alcock, S.E. and Cherry, J.F. (eds) (2004) *Side by Side Survey: Comparative Regional Studies in the Mediterranean World,* Oxford
Alcock, S.E., D'Altroy, T.N., Morrison, K.D., and Sinopoli, C.M. (eds) (2001) *Empires,* Cambridge
Ando, C. (2000) *Imperial Ideology and Provincial Loyalty in the Roman Empire* (Classics and Contemporary Thought No. 6), Los Angeles, Berkeley, and London
Bagnall, R.S. and Frier, B. (1994) *The Demography of Roman Egypt,* Cambridge
Ball, W. (2000) *Rome in the East. The Transformation of an Empire,* London
Balty, J. and Balty, J.-Ch. (1983) 'L'Apamène antique et les limites de la Syria Secunda', in T. Fahd (ed.) *La géographie administrative et politique d'Alexandre à Mahomet,* Leiden: 41-75
Barker, G. (1982) 'Economic life at Berenice: the animal and fish bones, marine molluscs and plant remains', in J.A. Lloyd (ed.) *Excavations at Sidi Khrebish Benghazi (Berenice),* Tripoli (Dept of Antiquities, Supplements to Libya Antiqua V): Vol II: 1- 49
Barker, G. (2000) 'Farmers, herders and miners in the Wadi Faynan, southern Jordan: a 10,000-year landscape archaeology', in Barker and Gilbertson 2000: 63-85
Barker, G. and Gilbertson, D.D. (eds) (2000) *Archaeology of Drylands: Living on the Margins,* London
Barker, G., Gilbertson, D., Jones, B. and Mattingly, D. (1996) *Farming the Desert.* Vol. 1: *Synthesis.* Vol. 2: *Gazeteer and Pottery,* Paris-Tripoli-London
Bauzou, T. (1998) 'Le secteur nord de la *via nova,* de Bostra à Philadelphie, in Humbert and Desreumaux 1998: 101-255
Beard, M. (1991) 'Writing and religion: *Ancient Literacy* and the function of the written word in Roman religion', in Humphrey 1991: 35-58
Bell, G. (1907) *The Desert and the Sown,* London
Bender, F. (1974) *Geology of Jordan,* Berlin

Bibliography

Bisheh, G. (1987) 'Qasr Mshatta in the light of a recently discovered inscription', *SHAJ* III: 193-7

Bookman (Ken-Tor), R., Enzel, Y., Agnon, A. and Stein, M. (2004) 'Late Holocene lake levels of the Dead Sea', *Geological Society of America Bulletin* May/ June 116.5/6: 555-71

Bottema, S. and van Zeist, W. (1981) 'Palynological evidence for the climatic history of the Near East, 50,000-65,000 BP', Colloques internationaux du CNRS 598, in *Préhistoire du Levant,* Paris: 111-32

Bowersock, G.W. (1983) *Roman Arabia,* Cambridge, MA

Bowersock, G.W. (1991) 'The Babatha Papyri, Masada and Rome', *JRA* 4: 336-44 (= Studies on the Eastern Roman Empire)

Bowman, A.K. (1991) 'Literacy in the Roman empire: mass and mode', in Humphrey 1991: 119-31

Bowman, A.K. (1991) and Wolf, G. (1994) *Literacy and Power in the Ancient World,* Cambridge

Broshi, M. (1980) 'The population of Western Palestine in the Roman-Byzantine period', *BASOR* 236: 1-10

Brown, P. (1999) 'Images as a substitute for writing', in E. Chrysos and I. Wood (eds) *East and West: Modes of Communication,* Leiden (Brill): 15-34

Brown, P. (2001) *Poverty and Leadership in the Later Roman Empire,* Hanover, NH

Burns, T.S. and Eadie, J.W. (2001) *Urban Centers and Rural Contexts in Late Antiquity,* Lansing, MI

Burton, G.P. (1975) 'Proconsuls, assizes and the administration of justice under the empire', *JRS* 65: 92-106

Butcher, K. (2003) *Roman Syria and the Near East,* London

Canova, R. (1954) *Iscrizioni e Monumenti Protocristiani del Paese di Moab,* Rome

Casson, L (1950) 'The Isis and her voyage', *TAPhA* 81: 43-56

Cotton, H.M. and Geiger, J. (1989) *Masada II. The Yigael Yadin Excavations 1963-1965. Final Reports: The Latin and Greek Documents,* Jerusalem

Cotton, H.M., Cockle, W.E.H. and Millar, F.G.B. (1995) 'The papyrology of the Roman Near East: a survey', *JRS* 85: 214-35

Dauphin, C. (1996) 'Baths, brothels and babes. Prostitution in the Byzantine Holy Land', *Classics Ireland* 3: 47-72

Dawes, E. and Baynes, N.H. (1948) *Three Byzantine Saints: Contemporary Biographies of St Daniel the Stylite, St Theodore of Sykeon and St John the Almsgiver,* tr. from the Greek, Oxford

De Vries, B. (1998) *Umm el-Jimal. A Frontier Town and its Landscape in Northern Jordan,* Portsmouth, RI (*JRA* Supp. 27)

Di Cosmo, N. (1994) 'Ancient inner Asian nomads: their economic basis

Bibliography

and its significance in Chinese history', *Journal of Asian Studies* 53.4: 1092-1126

Diamond, J. (1997) *Guns, Germs and Steel. A Short History of Everybody for the Last 13,000 Years,* London

Duncan-Jones, R. (1994) *Money and Government in the Roman Empire,* Cambridge

Dutton, R., Clarke, J. and Battikhi, A. (eds) (1998) *Arid Land Resources and their Management. Jordan's Desert Margin,* London

Dyson, S.L. (1989) 'Complacency and crisis in late twentieth century Classical archaeology', in P. Culham and L. Edmunds (eds) *Classics. A Discipline and Profession in Crisis?,* New York: 211-20

Dyson, S.L. (1993) 'From New to New-Age Archaeology: archaeological theory and Classical Archaeology – a 1990s perspective', *American Journal of Archaeology* 97: 195-206

Dyson, S.L. (2003) *The Roman Countryside,* London

Eck, W. (2002) 'Cheating the Public – or: Tacitus Vindicated', *SCI* 21, 2002, 149-64

Engels, D. (1999) *Classical Cats. The Rise and Fall of the Sacred Cat,* London

Enzel, Y., Bookman (Ken-Tor), R., Sharon, D., Gvirtzman, H., Dayan, U., Ziv, B. and Stein, M. (2003) 'Late Holocene climates of the Near East deduced from Dead Sea level variations and modern regional rainfall', *Quaternary Research* 60: 263-73

Evenari, M., Shannon, L. and Tadmor, N. (1971; 2nd edn 1982) *The Negev. The Challenge of a Desert,* Cambridge, MA

Feissel, D. and Gascou, J. (1989) 'Documents d'archives romains enédits du Moyen Euphrate (IIIe siècle apr. J.-C.)', *CRAI*: 535-61

Fink, R.O. (1971) *Roman Military Records on Papyrus,* Cleveland, OH

Foran, D., Harrison, T., Graham, A., Barlow, C. and Johnson, N.J. (2004) 'The Tell Madaba Archaeological Project: preliminary report of the 2002 field season', *ADAJ* 48: 7969-48

Foss, C. (1995) 'The Near Eastern countryside in Late Antiquity', in *The Roman and Byzantine Near East (I),* Ann Arbor, MI (*JRA* Supp. 14): 213-34

Freeman, P., Bennett, J., Fiema, Z.T. and Hoffman, B. (2002) *Limes XVIII. Proceedings of the XVIIIth International Congress of Roman Frontiers Studies held in Amman, Jordan. (September 2000),* 2 vols, Oxford (BAR Int. Series 1084)

Freeman-Grenville, G.S.P., Chapman, R.L. and Taylor, J.E. (2003) *The Onomasticon by Eusebius of Caesarea,* Jerusalem

Frere, S.S. (1987) *Britannia. A History of Roman Britain,* New York

Freyberger, K.S. (1992) 'Die Bauten und Bildwerke von Philippopolis: Zeugnisse imperialer und orientalischer Selbstdarstellung der Familie des Kaisers Philippus Arabs', *Damaszener Mitteilungen* 6: 293-311

Bibliography

Frézouls, E. (1989) 'Les edifices de spectacles en Syrie', in J.-M. Dentzer and W. Orthman (eds) (1989) *Archaéologie et histoire de la Syrie*, Saarbrucken

Frier, B. (2000) 'Demography', *CAH* XI: 787-816

Frier, B. (2001) 'More is worse: some observations on the population of the Roman empire', in Scheidel 2001b: 139-59

Garnsey, P. and Saller, R. (1987) *The Roman Empire Economy, Society and Culture*, London

Garrard, A.N., Byrd, B., Harvey, P. and Hivernel, F. (1985) 'Prehistoric environment and settlement in the Azraq Basin. A report on the 1982 survey season', *Levant* 17: 1-28

Gatier, P.-L. (1996) 'Gouverneurs et procurateurs à Gérasa', *Syria* 73: 47-56

Gerster, G. and Wartke, R.-B. (2003) *Flugbilder aus Syrien von der Antike bis zur Moderne*, Mainz

Gilbertson, D.D., Hunt, C.O., and Bradley, S. (1985) 'Micropalaeontological and palaeoecological studies of recent sediments from the Azraq marshes in the Jordanian Desert', *SHAJ* II: 347-52

Glueck, N. (1934-1951) *Explorations in Eastern Palestine, I-IV*, New Haven (AASOR XIV [1933-4]: 1-113; XV [1934-5]; XVIII-XIX [1937-9]; XXV-XXVIII [1945-9])

Goody, J.C. (ed.) (1968) *Literacy in Traditional Societies*, Cambridge

Graf, D. (2001) 'Town and countryside in Roman Arabia during Late Antiquity', in Burns and Eadie 2001: 219-40.

Graf, D.F. (1997c) *Rome and the Arabian Frontier: From the Nabataeans to the Saracens*, Aldershot (Variorum Series)

Grainger, J.D. (1990) *The Cities of Seleukid Syria*, Oxford

Habicht, C. (1975) 'New evidence on the province of Asia', *JRS* 65: 64-91

Haensch, R. (2002) Review of Lehmann and Holum 2000 in *SCI* 21 (2002): 323-7

Harris, W.V. (1989) *Ancient Literacy*, Cambridge, MA

Harrison, T., Foran, D., Graham, A., Griffith, T., Barlow, C. and Ferguson, J. (2003) 'The Tell Madaba Archaeological Project: preliminary report of the 1998-2000 field seasons', *ADAJ* 47: 129-48.

Häser, J. (2004) 'Ancient tunnel systems in northern Jordan', *SHAJ* 8: 155-9

Henige, D. (1998a) *Numbers From Nowhere. The American Indian Contact Population Debate*, Norman, OK

Henige, D. (1998b) 'He came, he saw, we counted: the historiography and demography of Caesar's Gallic numbers', *Annales de démographie historique 1998*: 215-42

Hirschfeld, Y. (1995) *The Palestinian Dwelling in the Roman-Byzantine Period*, Jerusalem

Bibliography

Hirschfeld, Y. (1997) 'Farms and villages in Byzantine Palestine', *DOP* 51: 33-71

Hirschfeld, Y. (2004) 'A climatic change in the early Byzantine period? Some archaeological evidence', *PEQ* 136: 133-49

Hirth, F. (1885) *China and the Roman Orient,* Shanghai and Hong Kong

Hopkins, K. (1978) 'Economic growth and towns in Classical Antiquity', in P. Abrams and E.A. Wrigley (eds) *Towns in Society. Essays in Economic History and Historical Sociology,* Cambridge: 35-77

Hopkins, K. (1980) 'Taxes and trade in the Roman empire', *JRS* 70: 101-25

Hopkins, K. (1991) 'Conquest by book', in Humphrey 1991: 133-58

Hopkins, K. (1999) 'Population', in Bowersock, G.W., Brown, P. and Grabar, O. (1999) *Late Antiquity. A Guide to the Post-Classical World,* Cambridge, MA: 646-7

Hopkins, K. (2002) 'Rome, taxes, rents and trade', in W. Scheidel and S. von Reden (eds), *Ancient Economy,* Edinburgh: 190-232

Horden, P. and Purcell, N. (2000) *The Corrupting Sea. A Study of Mediterranean History,* Oxford

Humbert, J.-B. and Desreumaux, A (1998) *Khirbet es-Samra, Jordanie. 1. La voie romaine; le cimetière; les documents épigraphiques,* Paris

Humphrey, J.H. (ed.) (1991) *Literacy in the Roman World,* Ann Arbor, MI (*JRA* Supp. 3)

Humphrey, J.H. (ed.) (1995) *The Roman and Byzantine Near East: Some New Archaeological Research, I* Ann Arbor (*JRA* Supp. 14)

Humphrey, J.H. (ed) (1999) *The Roman and Byzantine Near East, II,* Portsmouth, RI (*JRA* Supp. 31)

Huntington, E. (1924) *Civilization and Climate,* 3rd edn, New Haven, CT

Hütteroth, W. and Abdulfattah, K. (1977) *Historical Geography of Palestine, Transjordan and Southern Syria in the Late 16th Century,* Erlangen

Iliffe, J.H. (1945) 'Imperial art in Transjordan: figurines and lamps from a potter's store at Jerash', *QDAP* 11: 1-26

Irby, C.L. and Mangles, J. (1823) *Travels in Egypt and Nubia, Syria and Asia Minor During the Years 1817 and 1818,* London

Isaac, B. (1981) 'The Decapolis in Syria; a neglected inscription', *ZPE* 44: 67-74 (= Isaac 1998: 313-21 including 'Postscript')

Isaac, B. (1992) *The Limits of Empire. The Roman Army in the East,* rev. edn, Oxford

Isaac, B. (1994) 'Tax collection in Roman Arabia: a new interpretation of the evidence from the Babatha Archive', *Mediterranean Historical Review* 9: 256-66

Bibliography

Isaac, B. (1996) 'Eusebius and the geography of Roman provinces', in Kennedy 1996b: 153-67

Isaac, B. (1998) *The Near East Under Roman Rule. Selected Papers*, Leiden

Isaac, B. (2003) 'Latin and Greek in the inscriptions of Caesarea Maritima', *JRA* 16: 666-8 (Review of Lehmann and Holum)

Issar, A. and Zohar, M. (2004) *Climate Change – Environment and Civilization in the Middle East*, Berlin-Heidelberg-New York (Springer)

Jabbur, J.S. (1995) *The Bedouins and the Desert. Aspects of Nomadic Life in the Arab East*, New York

Johns, J. (1994) 'The longue durée: state and settlement strategies in Southern Transjordan across the Islamic centuries', in Rogan and Tell 1994: 1-10

Jones, A.H.M. (1971) *The Cities of the Eastern Roman Provinces*. 2nd edn, Oxford (Clarendon)

Jones, C.P. (1978) *The Roman World of Dio Chrysostom*, Oxford

Jones, R.F.J. (1977) 'A quantitative approach to Roman burial', in R. Reece (ed.) *Burial in the Roman World*, London (CBA Research Report 22): 20-5

Keay, S.J. (1988) *Roman Spain*, London

Kennedy, D.L. (1985) 'Ancient settlements in Syria', *Popular Archaeology*, September: 42-4

Kennedy, D.L. (1996a) 'Syria', *CAH* 10: 703-36

Kennedy, D.L. (1996b) *The Roman Army in the East*, Ann Arbor, MI (*JRA* Supp. 18)

Kennedy, D.L. (1997a) 'Aerial Archaeology in Jordan: air photography and the Jordanian Southern Hawran', in *SHAJ* VI: 77-86

Kennedy, D.L. (1997b) 'Roman roads and routes in north-east Jordan', *Levant* 29: 71-93

Kennedy, D.L. (1998a) 'The area of Umm el-Jimal: maps, air photographs and surface survey', in B. de Vries (ed.) *Umm el-Jimal, I: A Frontier Town and its Landscape in Northern Jordan*, Portsmouth, RI (*JRA* Supp. 26): 39-90

Kennedy, D.L. (1998b) 'The identity of Roman Gerasa: an archaeological approach', in G. Clarke (ed.) *Identities in the Eastern Mediterranean in Antiquity*, Sydney (Mediterranean Archaeology 11): 39-69 [published 1999]

Kennedy, D.L. (1999) 'Greek, Roman and native cultures in the Roman Near East', in Humphrey 1999: 76-106

Kennedy, D.L. (2000) 'The frontier of settlement in Roman Arabia. From Gerasa to Umm el-Jimal... and beyond', *Mediterraneo Antico* 2: 397-453

Kennedy, D.L. (2001a) 'Lessons from Libya: the impact of Rome', *Levant* 33: 205-8 (review of Barker 1996)

Bibliography

Kennedy, D.L. (2001b) 'History in depth: surface survey and aerial archaeology', in K. Amr (ed.) *SHAJ* VII: 39-48

Kennedy, D.L. (2001c) 'Khirbet Khaw: a Roman town and fort in northern Jordan', in N. Higham (ed.) *Archaeology of the Roman Empire: a tribute to the life and works of Professor Barri Jones,* Oxford (BAR, International Series 940): 173-88

Kennedy, D.L. (2002) 'Qaryat el-Hadid: A "lost" Roman military site in northern Jordan', *Levant* 34: 99-110

Kennedy, D.L. (2004a) 'Settlement in the Jarash Basin and its wider context. A proposal for fieldwork and a research project to interpret and explain settlement and landuse in Northwest Jordan', *SHAJ* VIII: 197-215

Kennedy, D.L. (2004b) *The Roman Army in Jordan,* 2nd edn, London

Kennedy, D.L. (2006a) 'The Roman Near East', *International History Review,* XXVIII.2: 353-68

Kennedy, D.L. (2006b) 'Demography, the population of Syria and the census of Q. Aemilius Secundus', *Levant* 38: 109-24

Kennedy, D.L. (forthcoming) 'Roads and routes in Northwest Jordan in the Roman period', in preparation

Kennedy, D.L. and Bewley, R. (2004) *Ancient Jordan from the Air,* London

Kennedy, D.L. and Freeman, P.W.M. (1995) 'Southern Hauran Survey 1992', *Levant* 27: 39-73

Kennedy, D.L and Riley, D.N. (1990) *Rome's Desert Frontier from the Air,* London

Kennedy. H. (1992) 'The impact of Muslim rule on the pattern of rural settlement in Syria', in Canivet, P. and Rey-Coquais, J.-P. (eds) (1992) *La Syrie de Byzance à l'Islam, VII-VIII Siècles: Actes du Colloque International,* Damascus (Institut Français de Damas): 291-7

Kermorvant, M., Leblanc, J. and Lenoir, M. (2003) 'Le camp de la legion IIIa Cyrenaica et sa zone d'activités', *Syria* 79: 134-40

Khazanov, A. (1994) *Nomads and the Outside World,* 2nd edn, Madison, WI

Koenen, L. and Kaimio, M. (1997) 'Report on decipherment of Petra Papyri (1996/97)', *ADAJ* 41: 459-62

Kraeling, C.H. (1938) *Gerasa: City of the Decapolis,* New Haven, CT

Krueger, D. (1996) *Symeon the Holy Fool: Leontius's Life and the Late Antique City,* Berkeley (Transformations of the Classical Heritage, XXV)

Lees, G.R. (1895) 'Across southern Bashan', *GJ* 5: 1-27

Lehmann, C.M. and Holum, K.G. (2000) *The Greek and Latin Inscriptions of Caesarea Maritima,* Boston, MA

Lentzen, C.J. and Knauf, A. (1987) 'Beit Ras/ Capitolias. A preliminary evaluation of the archaeological and textual evidence', *Syria* 64: 21-46

Lewis, D.M. (1994) 'The Persepolis tablets: speech, seal and script', in Bowman and Woolf 1994: 17-32

Lewis, N. (1974) *The Roman Principate: 27 B.C. – 285 A.D.*, Toronto (Hakkert)

Lewis, N. (ed.) (1989) *The Documents from the Bar Kokhba Period in the Cave of Letters: Greek Papyri. Aramaic and Nabatean Signatures and Subscriptions*, ed. Y. Yadin and J.C. Greenfield, Jerusalem (Israel Exploration Society and Hebrew University of Jerusalem)

Lewis, N.N. (1987) *Nomads and Settlers in Syria and Jordan, 1800-1980*, Cambridge

Ligt, L. de (1993) *Fairs and Markets in the Roman Empire. Economic and Social Aspects of Periodic Trade in a Pre-Industrial Society*, Amsterdam

Lo Cascio, E. (1994) 'The size of the Roman population: Beloch and the meaning of the Augustan census figures', *JRS* 84: 23-40

Lo Cascio, E. (2000) 'Population of Roman Italy in town and country', in Bintliff, J. and Sbonias. K. (eds) (2000) *Reconstructing Past Population Trends in Mediterranean Europe (3000 BC–AD 1800)*, Oxford (AML1): 161-71

Lo Cascio, E. (2001) 'Recruitment and the size of the Roman population from the third to the first centuries BC', in Scheidel 2001b: 111-37

Lucke, B. et al. (forthcoming) 'Soils and land use in the Decapolis region (Northern Jordan). Implications for landscape development and the impact of climate change', *ZDPV*

Lucke, B. Schmidt, M. Al-Saad, Z. Bens, O. Reinhard, F. Hüttl (2005) 'The abandonment of the Decapolis Region in Northern Jordan, forced by Environmental Change' *Quarternary International* 135: 65-91

MacAdam, H.I. (2002) *Geography, Urbanisation and Settlement Patterns in the Roman Near East*, Aldershot (Variorum Series)

MacAdam, H.I. and Graf, D.F. (1989) 'Inscriptions from the Southern Hauran Survey, 1985', *ADAJ* 33: 177-97; 288-394

MacCormack, S. (2001) 'Cuzco, another Rome?', in Alcock et al. 2001: 419-35

MacDonald, M.C.A. (1993) 'Nomads and the Hawran in the Late Hellenistic and Roman periods: a reassessment of the epigraphic evidence', *Syria* 70: 303-413

MacMullen, R. (1990) *Changes in the Roman Empire*, Princeton

Marshall, A.J. (1966) 'Governors on the move', *Phoenix* 20; 231-46

Matthews, J.F. (1984) 'The Tax Law of Palmyra. Evidence for economic history in a city of the Roman East', *JRS* 74: 157-80

Bibliography

McGing, B. (2002) 'Population and proselytism. How many Jews were there in the ancient world?', in J.R. Bartlett (ed.) *Jews in the Hellenistic and Roman Cities,* London: 88-106

McKitterick, R. (ed.) (1990) *The Uses of Literacy in Early Mediaeval Europe,* Cambridge

Millar, F. (1993) *The Roman Near East, 31 BC – AD 337,* Cambridge, MA

Millar, F.G.B. (1998) 'Caravan cities: The Roman Near East and long-distance trade by land', in M. Austin, J. Harries and C. Smith (eds) *Modus Operandi: Essays in Honour of Geoffrey Rickman,* 1998: 119-37

Millett, M. (1990) *The Romanization of Britain. An Essay in Archaeological Interpretation,* Cambridge

Moreland, J. (2001) *Archaeology and Text,* London

Moschos, St John (1992) *Spiritual Meadows,* Kalamazoo, MI (trans J. Wortley)

Mundy, M. (1996) 'Qada' 'Ajlun in the late nineteenth century: interpreting a region from the Ottoman land registers', *Levant* 28: 77-95

Newson, P. (2000) 'Differing strategies for water supply and farming in the Syrian Black Desert', in Barker and Gilbertson 2000: 86-102

Oliver, J.H. (1974) 'Minutes of a trial conducted by Caracalla at Antioch in AD 216', in *Mélanges helléniques offerts à Georges Daux,* Paris: 289-94

Osborne, R. (1987) *Classical Landscape With Figures,* London

Patlagean, E. (1977) *Pauvereté économique et pauvereté sociale à Byzance 4e – 7e siècles,* Paris

Pflaum, H.-G. (1955) 'Remarques sur l'onomastique de Castellum Celtianum', in E. Swoboda (ed.) *Carnuntina. Ergebnisse der Forschung über die Grenzprovinzen des römischen Reiches. Vorträge beim Internationalen Kongress der Altertumsforscher,* Carnuntum: 126-51

Piccirillo, M. (1993) *The Mosaics of Jordan,* Amman (ACOR Research Publication 1)

Pollard, N. (2000) *Soldiers, Cities, and Civilians in Roman Syria,* Ann Arbor, MI

Rathbone, D.W. (1990) 'Villages, land and population in Graeco-Roman Egypt', *PCPhS* 216: 103-42

Renfrew, C. and Bahn, P. (2004) *Archaeology,* 4th edn, London

Retzleff, A. and Mjely, A.M. (2004) 'Some inscriptions in the odeum at Gerasa (Jerash)', *BASOR* 336: 37-47

Riedl, N. (1999) 'Eine neu entdeckte Meilensteingruppe in Nordwestjordanien', *ZDPV* 115: 45-8

Robert, L. (1934) 'Inscription de Gérasa', *RPh* 8: 276-8 = *OMS* 1175-7

Rogan, E.L. (1994) 'Bringing the state back: the limits of Ottoman rule in Jordan, 1840-1910', in Rogan and Tell 1994: 32-57

Bibliography

Rogan, E.L. and Tell, T. (eds) (1994) *Village, Steppe and State: The Social Origins of Modern Jordan,* London

Roll, I. (2002) 'Crossing the Rift Valley: the connecting arteries between the road networks of Judaea-Palaestina and Arabia', in Freeman et al. 2002: 215-30.

Roll, I. (2005) 'Terrestrial transportation of the Roman army in the East. The case of Judaea/ Palaestina and its road network', in Visy 2005: 749-61

Rostovtzeff, M.I. (1932) *Caravan Cities,* Oxford

Roussel, P. and Visscher, F. de (1942-43) 'Les inscriptions de temple de Dmeir', *Syria* 23: 173-94

Rubin, R. (1989) 'The debate over climate changes in the Negev, 4th-7th centuries CE', *PEQ* 121: 71-8

Safrai, Z. (1994) *The Economy of Roman Palestine,* London

Sallares, R. (2002) *Malaria and Rome,* Oxford

Sartre, M. (1985) *Bostra. Des Origines à l'Islam,* Paris

Sartre, M. (1991) *L'Orient Romain. Provinces et sociétes provinciales en Méditerranée orientale d'Auguste aux Sévères (31 avant J.-C.– 235 après J.-C.),* Paris

Sartre, M. (2003) *D'Alexandre à Zénobie. Histoire du Levant antique IVe siècle av. J.-C. – IIIe siècle ap. J.-C.,* rev. edn, Paris

Sartre, M. (2005) *The Middle East Under Rome,* Cambridge, MA

Sauer, E.W. (ed.) (2004) *Archaeology and Ancient History: Breaking Down the Boundaries,* London and New York

Scheidel, W. (1994) 'Libitina's bitter gains: seasonal mortality and endemic disease in the ancient city of Rome', *Ancient Society* 25: 151-75

Scheidel, W. (2001a) *Death on the Nile. Disease and Demography of Roman Egypt,* Leiden (Mnemosyne 228)

Scheidel, W. (ed.) (2001b) *Debating Roman Demography,* Leiden (Mnemosyne 211)

Scheidel, W. (2003) 'Germs for Rome', in C. Edwards and G. Woolf (eds) *Rome the Cosmopolis,* Cambridge

Schürer, E. (1979) *The History of the Jewish People in the Age of Jesus Christ,* II, Edinburgh

Segal, A. (1995) *Theatres in Roman Palestine and Provincia Arabia,* Leiden

Seigne, J. (1985) 'Le sanctuare de Zeus à Jerash: éléments de chronologie', *Syria* 62: 287-95

Seigne, J. (1997) 'Les limites orientale et méridionale du territoire de Gerasa', *Syria* 74: 121-38

Seigne, J. (2002) 'A sixth century water-powered sawmill at Jarash', *ADAJ* 46: 205-13

Shahid, I. (1984a) *Rome and the Arabs,* Washington, D.C.

Bibliography

Shahid, I. (1984b) *Byzantium and the Arabs in the Fourth Century,* Washington, D.C.
Shahid, I. (1989) *Byzantium and the Arabs in the Fifth Century,* Washington, D.C.
Shahid, I. (1995) *Byzantium and the Arabs in the Sixth Century,* Washington, D.C.
Shaw, B.D. (1979) 'Rural periodic markets in Roman North Africa as mechanisms of social integration and control', in G. Dalton (ed.) *Research in Economic Anthropology. A Research Annual, 2,* Greenwich, Conn: 91-117
Shaw, B.D. (1981) 'Rural markets in North Africa and the political economy of the Roman Empire', *Antiquités Africaines* 17: 37-83 = Shaw 1995a: I
Shaw, B.D. (1995a) *Rulers, Nomads, and Christians in Roman North Africa,* Aldershot (Variorum)
Shaw, B.D. (1995b) *Environment and Society in Roman North Africa: Studies in History and Archaeology,* Aldershot (Variorum)
Shaw, B.D. (1996) 'Seasons of death: aspects of mortality in imperial Rome', *JRS* 86: 100-38
Shaw, B.D. (1997) 'Agrarian economy and the marriage cycle of Roman women', *JRA* 10: 57-76
Shaw, B.D. (2001a) 'The seasonal birthing cycle of Roman women', in Scheidel 2001b: 83-110
Shaw, B.D. (2001b) 'Challenging Braudel: a new vision of the Mediterranean', *JRA* 14: 419-53
Shaw, B.D. (2002) 'Loving the poor', *New York Review of Books,* 21 November 2001: 42-5
Shaw, B.D. (2003) 'Judicial nightmares and Christian memory', *Journal of Early Christian Studies* 11:4, 533-63
Shaw, B.D. (2006) *At the Edge of the Corrupting Sea,* Oxford
Sperber, D. (1998) *The City in Roman Palestine,* Oxford
Spijkerman, A. (1978) *The Coins of the Decapolis and Provincia Arabia,* Jerusalem
Stiller, M., Ehrlich, A., Pohlinger, U., Baruch, U. and Kaufman, A. (1983-8) 'The Late Holocene sediments of Lake Kinneret (Israel) – multidisciplinary study of a five meter core', *GSI Current Research Report*: 83-8
Storey, G.R. (1997) 'Estimating the population of ancient Roman cities', in R.R. Paine (ed.) *Integrating Archaeological Demography: Multidisciplinary Approaches to Prehistoric Population,* Carbondale, IL
Taylor, J. (2002) *Petra and the Lost Kingdom of the Nabataeans,* London
Thompson, H.A. (1987) 'The impact of Roman architects and architecture on Athens, 170 BC – AD 170', in S. Macready and F.H. Thompson (eds) *Roman Architecture in the Greek World,* London: 1-17

Bibliography

Touchan, R. and Hughes, M. (1999) 'Dendrochronology in Jordan', *Journal of Arid Environments* 42: 291-303
Visy, Z. (2005) *Limes XIX. Proceedings of the XIXth International Congress of Roman Frontier Studies*, Pecs
Wahlin, L. (1997) 'The family cistern: 3000 years of household water collection in Jordan', in M. Sabour and K. Vikor (eds), *Ethnic Encounters and Culture Change*, Bergen (Nordic Society for Middle Eastern Studies): 233-49
Walmsley, A.G. and Damgaard, K. (2005) 'The Umayyad congregational mosque of Jarash in Jordan and its relationship to early mosques', *Antiquity* 79: 362-78
Watson, P. (2004) 'Cultural identity and wine production in northern Jordan: a case study in context', in *SHAJ* VIII: 485-502
Weber, T. (2000) 'Roman monumental arches in the Near East. Monuments of civic representation or custom toll stations', *SHAJ* VII: 531-6
Weiss, P. and Speidel, M.P. (2005) 'Das erste Militärdiplome für Arabia', *ZPE* 150: 253-64
Weiss, Z. (1999) 'Adopting a novelty: the Jews and the Roman games in Palestine', in Humphrey 1999: 23-49
Welles, C.B., Fink, R.O. and Gilliam, J.F. (1959) *The Excavations at Dura-Europos. Final Report V.1 The Parchments and Papyri*, New Haven, CT
Whittaker, C.R. (1993) 'The poor', in A. Giardina (ed.) *The Romans*, Chicago: 272-99
Whittow, M. (1999) 'Rome and the Jafnids: writing the history of a 6th-c tribal dynasty', in Humphrey 1999: 207-24
Wilkinson, T. J. (2003) 'Archaeological survey and long-term population trends in Upper Mesopotamia and Iran', in N.F. Miller and K. Abdi (eds) *Yeki Bud, Yeki Nabud: Essays on the Archaeology of Iran in Honor of William M. Sumner* (Monograph, Cotsen Institute of Archaeology), Los Angeles: 39-51
Wootton, G. (2000) *Monuments as Evidence for the Essence of Roman Popular Mime and its Diffusion throughout the Roman Empire*, 2 vols, unpub. PhD thesis (University of Western Australia)
Wrigley, E.A. (1983) 'The growth of population in eighteenth-century England: a conundrum resolved', *Past and Present* 98: 121-50 (= E.A. Wrigley (ed.) *People, Cities and Wealth*, Oxford: 215-41)
Wrigley, E.A. (1998) 'Explaining the rise in marital fertility in England in the "long" eighteenth century', *EHR* 51: 435-64
Young, G.K. (2001) *Rome's Eastern Trade. International Commerce and Imperial Policy 31 BC – AD 305*, London
Zanker, P. (2000) 'The city as symbol: Rome and the creation of an urban image', in Fentress, E. (ed.) (2000) *Romanization and the City: Creations, Transformations, and Failures*, Portsmouth, RI (*JRA* Supp. 38): 25-41

Indexes

Place-names

Abila (Qweilbeh), 16, 30-1, 34, 51, 111, 118, 120, 156, 193
Abila (Peraea) (Tell al-Kuffrein?), 31, 111
Adraha (Dera'a), 16, 31, 53, 111, 118, 120, 160, 194
Africa, Roman North, 42, 52, 178, 179, 180
Aila, 118
Ajlun, Highlands of, 15, 16, 18, 21, 43, 50, 53, 55, 56, 57, 60, 62, 67, 68, 77, 88, 89, 93, 96, 98, 104, 156, 174, 185, 186, 191
Alexandria, 110
Amman, see Philadelphia
Antioch, 84, 112, 135, 153, 159, 172, 180, 187
Apamea (Syria), 84, 95, 110-13, 117, 120
Aphaca, 181
Arabia, province of, 16, 19, 20, 21, 37, 113, 115, 118, 120, 130, 131, 132, 133, 134, 152, 156, 160, 162, 164, 165, 168, 169, 170, 180
Arbela (Irbid?), 111
Asia, 157-8
Athens, 39
Azraq, 103
Azraq (Oasis, Basin), 18, 21, 31, 55, 56, 57, 70, 74, 92, 93, 94, 95, 146, 192, 196
Baetocaece, 180
Batnae, 179, 180
Belqa, 43, 45, 48, 50, 56, 57, 60, 62, 67, 71, 96, 102, 104
Beit Ras, see Capitolias
Beth Shean, see Scythopolis
Besimoth, 16, 31, 85, 111, 193
Biqa Valley, Lebanon, 62
Bosra, see Bostra
Bostra (Bosra), 16, 18, 26, 30-1, 34, 35, 36, 57, 76, 86, 89, 91, 92, 105, 111, 112, 113, 118, 120, 121, 155, 157, 159-62, 165, 172, 177, 193
Britain, 114-15, 135, 167
Caesarea Maritima, 35, 159, 161
Capitolias (Beit Ras), 30, 34, 111
Characmoab (Kerak), 44, 118
China, 47, 152, 179
Dafyaneh, 121
Damascus, 15, 100, 187
Dead Sea, 54-7, 60, 77, 79-81, 83
Decapolis, 16, 30, 50, 71, 111-12, 123, 154, 196
Deir el-Kahf, 31, 92
Dera'a, see Adraha
Dion, 111
Dura Europos, 130, 134, 136, 147, 166, 179, 184
Egypt, 28, 44, 86, 110, 115, 119, 128, 129, 131-2, 134, 135, 138, 147, 158, 159, 163, 167-9, 175, 180-1

211

Indexes

Emesa (Homs), 125, 182
Ephesus, 158, 181
Esbus (Hisban), 16, 31, 57, 58, 71, 76, 92, 111, 117, 118, 120, 193
El-Fedein, 103
Gadara (Umm Qeis), 30, 34, 57, 71, 76, 86, 91, 111, 123, 140, 154, 156, 159-60, 165, 172, 180, 183, 193
Gadora (Salt), 31, 34, 104-5, 107, 111, 193-4
Galilee, Sea of, 53, 60, 79, 81, 83, 152-3
Gerasa (Jarash), 16, 18, 21, 23, 26, 30-1, 34-5, 36, 38-40, 41, 43, 46, 56, 57, 68, 69-74, 76, 84, 86, 88, 96, 98, 101, 102, 111, 112, 113, 116, 117, 118, 120, 123, 124, 125, 130, 131, 132, 134, 135, 140, 146, 156, 159, 160, 162, 165, 168, 170, 172, 177, 180, 181, 182, 186, 193
Gulf, 19, 51, 55, 187, 189
Hallabat, *see* Qasr el-Hallabat
Hauran (*see also* Southern Hauran), 43, 45, 86, 95, 96, 102, 105, 140, 144, 147, 149
Hayyan al-Mashrif, 23
Hebron, 180
Hedjaz, 154
Hisban, *see* Esbus
Hula, Lale, 81, 83
Imtan, 91, 92
Inat, 93
Irbid, *see* Arbela
Israel, 35, 79, 82, 83, 192
Italica, 39
Jarash, *see* Gerasa
Jarash Basin, 68, 69, 70, 192
Jarash, Wadi, 68, 70, 116
Jarash, Tall, 84, 88
Jauf (Dumata), 92, 94
Jimal, *see* Umm el-Jimal

Jiza (Zizia), 57, 73
Jordan, 44, 51
Judaea (*see also* Palaestina), 115, 119-20, 129, 131, 153, 158, 159, 161, 165, 167, 176
Jordan River/Valley, 53, 55, 56, 60, 67, 76
Khan es-Zebib, 103
Khirbet Khaw, 31-2, 98
Khirbet es-Samra, 23, 36, 194
Korykos, 177
Lepcis Magna, 38-40, 46
Libya, 22, 38, 42-3, 45, 52, 193
Livias (Tell er-Rama), 31, 111
Madaba (Madaba), 16, 26, 31, 57, 71, 76, 86, 107, 111, 118, 120, 165, 193
Madaba Plain, 48, 57, 58, 73
Masada, 78, 79, 131
Moab, 148, 155, 161
Mujib, Wadi, 54, 55, 56, 81, 88, 152
Nabataean Kingdom, Nabataeans, 85, 89, 93, 105, 131, 144, 145, 146, 147, 154-5, 161, 168, 183
Negev Desert, 68, 96, 99, 154
Ostia, 116
Palaestina (*see also* Judaea), 131, 156, 161, 165, 175
Palmyra, 60, 180, 181, 196
Pella (Tabaqat Fihl), 16, 26, 30-1, 76, 84, 89, 91, 111, 118, 120, 159, 160, 165, 183, 193
Peraea, 16, 31, 85, 92, 93, 152, 153, 193
Petra, 118, 131, 133, 140, 147, 155, 161, 165, 168, 184
Philadelphia (Amman, Rabbath Ammon), 16, 30-1, 34, 35, 36, 53, 54, 57, 71, 76, 89, 96, 103, 111, 112, 128, 156, 165, 182, 183, 194
Philippopolis (Shahba), 39, 46
Pompeii, 119-20, 147, 177

Indexes

Qaryat el-Hadid, 32
Qasr Ain es-Sil, 103
Qasr Amra, 103
Qasr el-Hallabat, 17-18, 19, 57, 71, 73, 76, 90, 91, 92, 93, 102, 103, 194
Qasr el-Kharaneh, 103
Qasr Mshatta, 103
Qasr Mushash, 103
Qasr et-Tuba, 103
Qasr el-Uweinid, 93
Qastal, 103
'Qubbash', 45, 103
Qweilbeh, see Abila
Rabba, see Rabbathmoab
Rabbathmoab, 118, 132, 165, 168
Rihab, 18, 23, 71, 89, 98, 112, 194
Rome (city of), 108, 116, 124, 139, 140, 157, 158, 159, 162, 175, 177
Sabah, 121
Salcha (Salkhad), 91, 92, 121
Salt, see Gadora
Samra, see Khirbet es-Samra
Scythopolis (Beth Shean), 16, 30, 31, 76, 89, 111, 156, 159, 160, 165, 193
Shahba, see Philippopolis
Shallalah, Wadi esh-, 53, 76
Sirhan, Wadi, 57, 196
Southern Hauran (*see also* Hauran), 18, 21, 35, 45, 55, 60, 62, 68, 72, 73, 74, 93, 105, 106, 113, 121, 132, 135, 192
Syria, 21, 39, 43, 45, 47, 55, 60, 62, 84, 85, 86, 95, 102, 111, 112, 115, 116, 119, 128, 130, 134, 143, 153, 156, 158, 159, 167, 169, 180, 195, 197
Syrian Desert, 51, 60
Tabaqat Fihl, see Pella
Tell al-Kuffrein, see Abila (Peraea)
Tell er-Rama, see Livias
Tetrapolis, 112
Tiberias, 76
Umm el-Jimal, 18, 21, 23, 32-3, 35, 36, 73, 76, 93, 94, 98, 99, 111, 113, 119, 120, 121, 146, 172, 192, 194
Umm el-Walid, 103
Umm Qeis, see Gadara
Umm el-Quttein, 34, 74, 89-93, 121, 146, 149
Umm er-Resas, 96-7, 98, 194
Umm es-Surab, 121, 194
Yajuz, 96-7
Yarmuk, Wadi, 53, 54, 55, 76, 81, 152, 156
Zarqa, 34, 57, 93, 98
Zarqa, River (Wadi), 53, 76, 85
Zodocatha, 184

People

Abbassids, 45
Aemilius Secundus, Q., 110-11
Avilius Flaccus, 158
Babatha, see Subjects: Babatha Archive
Ghassanids, 41, 44
Hadrian, 39, 40, 158, 165, 182
Herod Agrippa I, 158, 159
Herod the Great, 35, 85, 152-4
Philip, 39
Septimius Severus, 39
Umayyads, 15, 23, 45, 76, 96, 99, 100-5, 109, 121, 186

213

Indexes

Subjects

Aerial Archaeology, 22, 23, 24, 25, 32, 34, 98-9, 105, 114, 125, 191, 192
air photographs, *see* Aerial Archaeology
amphitheatre, 30-1
archives, 128-34, 137, 140, 147, 163, 165, 168, 169, 183
army, Roman, 19, 26, 37, 89, 92-3, 112, 113-15, 118, 120, 129, 130, 136, 139-40, 146, 148, 155, 161, 166-7, 183, 194, 197
assizes, 139, 162-6, 172, 179
Babatha Archive, 130-4, 140, 142, 147, 165, 168, 169, 183
baths, 102, 172, 177, 178
beduin, 44-9, 68, 72
boundaries, provincial, 152-6
boundary markers, 105, 112, 136
'Byzantine boom', 45
bridge, 76, 88, 91, 94
Carolingian Empire, 142-3, 149
cats, 172
cemetery, 23, 36, 123-5, 137, 149
census, 27, 36, 111, 120, 131, 132-4, 137, 138, 140, 164, 166, 167-70
Christianity, 104, 141, 173
churches, 23, 95-100, 101, 112, 129, 133, 149, 185, 186, 187, 194
circus, *see* hippodrome
cisterns, 73-5, 98, 106
cities, 16, 23, 116-20, 171, 185, 187, 193, 196
city population, 120-1, 123
city walls, 112, 113, 116, 117, 119, 137
Classical Archaeology, 24-6, 29
climate, 51, 77-82, 188, 192-3, 197

communication, 22, 47, 52, 53-5, 67, 74-7, 88-94, 126-50, 162, 186, 190
comparative evidence, 42-9
connect(ivity), 50, 52
construction, monumental, 41, 86-8, 100, 101, 185
cultural identity, 21
'Dead Cities' (Syria), 95
Desert (Basalt, Chert), 18, 51, 55, 56, 57, 68, 92, 94, 99, 102, 136, 143, 145, 186, 192
economy (*see also* markets), 131, 164-5, 174, 176, 189-90, 196
empires, 20, 26, 47, 52, 128, 188-9
environment, 22, 24, 47, 50-83, 77-82, 192-3
estates (*see also* imperial and royal estate), 130
evidence, 28-37
fair, 179, 180
farms, farming, 22, 39, 43, 46, 49, 52, 67-74, 98-100, 194, 196
fields, 68, 70, 72, 94, 99, 105, 106, 173
food, 67, 70, 117, 119, 120, 131, 171-3, 174, 189
forts, 31-4, 92, 109, 146
geography, 50-83
government and administration, Ottoman, 43, 46, 48
government and administration, Roman, 35, 38, 155-6, 156-67
graffiti (*see also* 'Safaitic' inscriptions), 28, 129, 135, 137, 147
ground survey, 22-3, 24-5, 42, 44, 45, 84, 85, 102, 106, 191-3, 196
health and disease, 171-3, 175, 184

Indexes

hippodrome, 30-1
Horden and Purcell, *The Corrupting Sea*, 15, 22, 52, 62, 67
houses, 23, 96, 98, 102, 113, 116, 118, 119, 120, 137, 173, 178, 184, 192, 193
immigrants, 44, 105
imperial and royal estate, 45, 104-7, 130
inn, 177-8
inscriptions (*see also* 'Safaitic', Syro-Palestinian, tombstones), 23, 28-9, 31, 34-6, 39, 40, 42, 112, 123-4, 167, 175, 177, 179-80, 194
Islam, 20, 23, 45, 79, 100-3, 104, 182, 185, 186, 187
Jews, 84, 1110, 123, 125, 130, 141
'kites', 18, 23, 106, 192
land holding/ tenure, 104, 130, 132, 134, 137, 145, 183, 184
languages, 23, 34, 35, 42, 123, 126-50 *passim*, 168, 185, 189
latrine, 171, 173
library, *see* archives
literacy, 126-50
Long Classical Millennium (LCM), 15, 185, 191
markets, 42, 139, 178, 179-80, 185
'Melkite' inscriptions, *see* Syro-Palestinian inscriptions
methodologies, 37-49
micro-regions, 50, 62-74
milestones, 88-95, 130, 136, 139, 142, 146, 149, 161, 187
mosaics, 23, 28, 76, 96, 98, 100, 102, 112, 129, 142, 149, 178, 187
mosque, 102, 187
names, 182-3
Near East, *see* Roman Near East

nomads, 20-1, 40-9, 68, 70, 95, 105, 143-7, 186, 195-6
occupations, 135, 176-9, 189
Ottoman records, 43, 195
Pax Romana, 188, 190
Petra Papyri, 131, 133-4, 147, 184
pollen analysis, 78, 79, 83
population, 108-25, 189, 190-1
population density, 116-20
pottery (ceramics), 29, 44
poverty, 171-4
pre-desert (steppe), 20, 56, 57, 60, 77, 121
procurator, 160, 161, 162
Princeton Expeditions to Syria (PES), 32, 35, 96
prostitution, 177-8, 179, 180
provinces, 151-6
rats, 171-2
religion (temples, shrines; *see also* churches), 20, 133, 134, 135, 137, 140, 180, 181, 182, 185, 187
reservoirs, 73, 74, 102, 106, 186
rituals of life (birth, marriage, death), 174-6, 190
roads and tracks (*see also Via Nova Traiana, 'Via Severiana'*), 23, 49, 76, 88-95, 100, 109, 130, 136, 145, 146, 149, 186, 194
Roman Empire (character and workings), 26, 37-8
Roman Empire (population size), 108, 114
Roman Near East, 19, 25
sacrifices and offerings, 134, 136, 180-2
'Safaitic' inscriptions, 18, 42, 95, 129, 136, 142-7, 148, 186, 197
settlement, 15-19, 20, 23, 24, 26, 42, 43-4, 84-107, 109, 112, 185-6, 187, 188, 194
soils, 51, 60-2, 68, 70, 82

Indexes

statues, 129, 131, 137, 162, 180
steppe, *see* pre-desert
survey, *see* ground survey
Syro-Palestinian ('Melkite') inscriptions, 23, 36, 115, 129, 142
tax, 29, 44, 46, 49, 132-3, 137-9, 164, 180, 190
territory, 112
theatre, 30-1, 86-7, 137, 185, 193
tombstones/ epitaphs, 23, 29, 36, 89, 123-4, 129, 130, 137, 142, 146-9, 182, 184
trade, traders, 19, 20, 39, 46, 55, 95, 100, 135, 141, 144, 179, 181, 187, 189, 190, 195-6
transport, 55, 67, 100, 169
travellers, early modern, 47-9, 76, 107
tree-rings, 78-9, 192
Umayyad mansions, 102-4, 186
UNESCO Libyan Valleys Survey, 42, 193

urban : rural population, 109, 117, 123
vegetation and agriculture, 62-6
'*Via Militaris*', 196
Via Nova Traiana, 32, 35, 76, 89, 165, 196
'*Via Severiana*', 92
villages, 18, 22, 29, 42, 44, 45, 47, 57, 72, 85, 95-100, 105, 109, 113, 116, 119, 121, 123, 125, 130, 132, 140, 143, 146-7, 149, 172, 174, 179, 180, 185, 186, 194, 197
'virtual island', 15, 22, 50, 52-5, 124, 185
water, 19, 51, 55, 57-60, 67-74, 172, 173
water-harvesting, cross wadi walls, 19, 68, 72-7, 82, 99, 106, 186
wine, 172
writing, 28-9, 126-50, 187, 189-90
writing materials, 129-31